W9-CSU-984

Novell Certification Handbook

Novell Certification Handbook

John Mueller, CNE

Robert A. Williams, CNE, CNI

Windcrest®/McGraw-Hill

New York San Francisco Washington, D.C. Auckland Bogotá
Caracas Lisbon London Madrid Mexico City Milan
Montreal New Delhi San Juan Singapore
Sydney Tokyo Toronto

pbk 3 4 5 6 7 8 9 10 11 FGR/FGR 9 9 8 7 6 5 4
hc 3 4 5 6 7 8 9 10 11 FGR/FGR 9 9 8 7 6 5 4

Library of Congress Cataloging-in-Publication Data
Mueller, John, 1958–
    Novell certification handbook / by John Mueller, Robert A.
Williams.
      p. cm.
    Includes index.
    ISBN 0-8306-4555-1 (pbk.)   ISBN 0-8306-4554-3 (H)
    1. Electronic data processing personnel—Certification.
  2. Novell, Inc. I. Williams, Robert A. (Robert Allen) II. Title.
  HD8039.D37M84   1993
  004'.023'73—dc20   93-29457
                                                                        CIP

Acquisitions editor: Brad J. Schepp
Editorial team: Laura J. Bader, Book Editor
                Susan Wahlman, Managing Editor
                Joanne Slike, Executive Editor
                Joann Woy, Indexer
Production team: Katherine G. Brown, Director
                Ollie Harmon, Coding
                Tina M. Sourbier, Coding
                Brenda S. Wilhide, Layout
                Cindi Bell, Proofreading
Design team: Jaclyn J. Boone, Designer
                Brian Allison, Associate Designer
Cover design: Carol Stickles, Allentown, Pa.   WU1
                                                                4494

Dedication

This book is dedicated to our families. Like the network administrator who spends the weekend searching frantically for that broken cable, our families had to spend many weekends without us as we put this book together. Both of us would like to thank our wives, Rebecca and Cyndie, for their endless support, tireless resolve to keep our homes together, and loving care when things didn't go well.

Contents

Introduction

The *Novell Certification Handbook* is the one source of information you
need to prepare for, obtain, and use any of the certifications offered by
Novell. Many network administrators need to get their certification, but
they are unaware of the requirements or unsure of who to contact. This
book provides you with all the answers you need to improve your job
performance by getting a Novell certification.

Of course, improving job performance is one step toward many goals. For
example, you might want a job with more responsibility, better pay, or
greater advancement potential. The *Novell Certification Handbook* helps
you gain these goals by showing you how to present your certification to
potential employers or clients. Learning how to present your certification
is as important as getting it in the first place. In total, this book helps you
in 10 specific ways.

1. Learn the differences between the various certifications offered by
   Novell: Certified NetWare Administrator (CNA), Certified NetWare
   Engineer (CNE), Enterprise Certified NetWare Engineer (ECNE),
   and Certified NetWare Instructor (CNI). Many users are unsure
   what level or type of certification they need. Especially unclear are
   the differences between CNE and ECNE. This book helps you
   understand the differences and plan for the level of certification
   that meets your needs.

2. Enhance your career by getting a Novell certification today. Many
   people face a Novell certification as an extra responsibility they
   neither want nor need. The *Novell Certification Handbook* can help
   you over this hurdle by showing you the benefits of such a
   certification. In many cases a positive attitude can mean the
   difference between getting and not getting certified.

3. Plan for the certification process. It's unfortunate, but many people
   start CNA or CNE training with no idea of what to expect or how to
   prepare for it. In some instances the person has never even used a
   computer before, but now he or she must learn to run a network. The
   Novell Certification Handbook can help you prepare for certification
   by explaining the certification requirements. It also helps you create a
   checklist tailored to your needs. Writing down what you need to do is
   at least half the battle in planning for certification.

4. Understand what support you can expect from Novell. Part of the
   benefit of getting certified is the support that Novell provides. While
   the documentation provided with the certification package outlines

some of the benefits, a mere list is not enough. This book shows you what you can do with these additional support items.

5. Plan for continuing education requirements. Many people approach a Novell certification as they would a high school education. Once it's over, they peacefully go back to their old routine, never acknowledging the need to continue their education. Fortunately, the Novell recertification requirements quickly make these people aware of the need for continuing education. This book can help you prepare for it before you lose your certification because of a lack of planning.

6. Find all your certification questions answered in one place. One of the big problems in getting a Novell certification is that you can spend many hours searching for answers to your questions. This problem isn't new or unique; colleges and universities face the same problem. Many authors have addressed the issues of getting from point A to point B in these institutions. For example, just look at all the books that tell you how to get a GED or take a SAT test, both requirements for getting into a college or university. Currently there is no guide for people who want to become a CNE; this book answers that need.

7. Get your certification quickly and easily. This book provides tips and hints that reduce the chance of failure when taking a test, possibly saving days or even weeks in the certification process. Add to this the time saved researching the certification itself and you could end up saving a month or more in the certification cycle.

8. Learn what courses are available. Many people miss opportunities to learn something they really wanted to know about NetWare simply because they don't know what courses are available. The *Novell Certification Handbook* provides a list of classes provided by Novell. All you need to do is decide which courses you want to take (as long as they meet certification requirements), sign up, and take the courses.

9. Get answers to your questions quickly and easily. The *Novell Certification Handbook* provides a list of important phone numbers that you can call whenever you need help with a problem. Instead of writing these numbers on scraps of paper that invariably get lost when you really need them, you can get help quickly by using this guide. In addition, instead of playing telephone tag with the one person you thought could help, only to find out he or she can't, this book helps you find the right person the first time.

10. Find sources of additional information. No one book has a solution to every problem. Rather than strand you without the resources you need, this book provides a list of places you can go for additional help. This resource is very important to both the novice and the expert reader.

Many people don't understand what a Novell certification is or why they need it, including employers and clients. Even if you understand why the certification is important, presenting these facts to an employer or client can prove difficult. The *Novell Certification Handbook* provides you with a full description of each of the certifications and why they are important. It not only increases your own knowledge, but helps you explain it to potential clients and employers as well. Knowing this information could mean the difference between getting a job or losing it to someone less qualified than yourself. It also helps you get the level of compensation you deserve for having a certification.

Why you need certification

This book provides you with all the information you need to get and use your certification. We start by telling you why you need the certification, proceed with educational requirements, then tell you about testing requirements. The *Novell Certification Handbook* even tells you how to add your certification to your resume and how to present it to a potential employer. The book ends with a section on continuing education requirements. The following paragraphs tell you about the contents of each chapter.

What this book contains

Everyone needs to learn about the basics before they can start a new task. Getting a Novell certification isn't any different. This chapter explains what types of certifications Novell offers, what differentiates them from other certifications, and the criteria for getting the certification. The most important feature of this chapter is that it tells you all about the duties and responsibilities associated with the various certifications. This allows you to focus on the certification you actually require to get your job done, rather than trying to figure out what you need based on course outlines.

Chapter 1— Getting started

Once you figure out which certification to get, the chapter helps you design a checklist for your particular certification course. Since each person starts at a different knowledge threshold, each company's requirements are different, and Novell offers elective courses in some areas, your checklist will contain unique requirements.

Every person needs to look at different aspects of the certification process. This book helps you tailor a certification map that meets your specific needs. Rather than use a generic map that someone else created, you can forge your own road through the certification jungle. Of course, forging your own path takes more time and effort, but it pays in the long run because you'll know how to use your certification better.

This book helps you see what roadblocks you'll face and how to avoid them. It also helps you create your certification map faster and more accurately. Mistakes cost time; this book can help you prevent certification mistakes that could add weeks or even months to your certification effort. The checklists and other organizational aids help you get organized quickly.

Chapter 2—Understanding the certification process

Once you gain a full appreciation of what the certification accomplishes, you can concentrate on how certification helps you on the job. This chapter answers questions like, "Why is certification important?" Once you understand this concept, you can take a detailed look at the certification requirements. This will help you complete the certification checklist you started in chapter 1. This chapter also helps you schedule the time required to complete the certification. Some participants in the certification process never get certified because they don't schedule the time required to complete the process. The guidelines in this chapter help reduce the probability of such an occurrence.

Chapter 3—Learning the trade

After you get all the planning done, it's time to get the required training. Currently some candidates choose to avoid training classes altogether. At an average cost of $600, it's not too difficult to figure out why they would want to do so. Unfortunately, it's these people who usually end up dropping out or taking the classes anyway. Rather than waste your time and effort trying to take the tests without the proper training, it's to your benefit to take the courses. This chapter helps explain the need for training and what goals you should set as part of the training process. It also helps you see instances where you could take a test immediately instead of going through a class first. Finally, the book takes a look at what you can do to get the maximum benefit from your training experience.

Chapter 4—Taking the tests

Taking tests is the least favorite part of any training experience. Professional examinations are more difficult than just about any other examination you can take. Novell's examinations are no different. Even if you go through all the training courses, study hard, and take the proper approach to testing, there is a good chance you will fail at least one examination. This chapter covers these areas by telling you how to study and what to study. It also stresses the importance of taking the Novell viewpoint when answering questions. Most important of all, this chapter helps you over the ultimate hurdle, dealing with failure. The better prepared the person taking the test is, the more devastating the failure becomes. Helping you get back on your feet is a very important feature of this book.

The job's never finished until the paperwork's done. This is a truism for Novell certification as well. Even if you finish all the required tests and training, you can still fumble around for several weeks just getting all the paperwork finished. The problem is that Novell lacks a written procedure for getting this paperwork finished. This chapter deals with this problem by providing you with step-by-step instructions on filling out the paperwork and getting all the required documentation together. It also provides you with a list of people you need to talk with and whom you need to send the paperwork to. Finally, it tells you what kind of paperwork you should get back from Novell and how long it usually takes to receive it.

Chapter 5—Getting the paperwork finished

Gaining access to a skill is only the first step in using it as a career enhancing tool. This chapter helps you understand what you need to do to use the certification you acquire to your benefit. This particular chapter focuses on the individual working for someone else. We cover a number of topics, from advancing in your current company to getting a new (and hopefully better) job based on that training.

Chapter 6—Using your certification to your advantage

The bottom line in getting certified is enhanced job opportunities. Certification can allow you to get a job with higher pay and to perform more interesting work. Why make every day a boring trek to the same old work? This book shows you how to use that certification to make life interesting and your work more profitable.

All Novell certifications require some maintenance. Lack of maintenance is the number one reason that people lose their certification. Every time Novell releases a new NetWare product, the certificate holder must take another test proving their proficiency with that product. Even though the time allotted to perform this task is usually more than sufficient, many people fail to make the grade because of a lack of planning. This chapter emphasizes two forms of continuing education. The first is professional-level training. It answers questions like, "What types of new equipment is the industry creating?" The second is Novell specific. It helps you prepare for and pass the recertification examination. This chapter also helps you see the importance of both types of continuing education.

Chapter 7—Planning for continuing education requirements

Many consultants make a living installing and maintaining Novell networks. This chapter specifically targets the networking expert. It provides the consultant with ideas on how they can improve their business through proper use of Novell supplied aids. It also examines some of the ways that the consultant can use a certification to gain and keep new clients. Finally, this chapter examines some thorny issues like what to charge the client for network services and how to maintain a professional relationship with the client.

Chapter 8—The consulting approach

1 Getting started

Everyone needs to learn the basics before they start a new task. Getting a Novell certification isn't any different. This chapter explains what types of certifications Novell offers, what differentiates them from other certifications, and the criteria for getting the certification. All the duties and responsibilities associated with the various certifications are also discussed. We even include a procedure for creating your own certification checklist, a must for anyone serious about obtaining this useful and beneficial credential.

Novell patterned its certification process after the credit system used by colleges. Each exam passed earns a predetermined number of credit points. There are two types of credits: required and elective. The required credits cover the base or core exams, while the elective credits allow you to pick the exams that are in your field of expertise or that interest you. Each certification requires a certain number of both required and elective credits.

Novell offers four classes of certification: CNA, CNE, ECNE, and CNI. All four certifications lend credibility to self and valuable knowledge to your work habits. As you understand what each certification requires, you will be able to select the one that is right for your knowledge and experience level.

What is a CNA?

The Certified NetWare Administrator (CNA) is Novell's entry-level certification. It is for the person who needs to administer a network on a day-to-day basis. Often the duties of this person include adding users, assigning security to the users, writing login scripts, backing up the system, installing applications onto the network, and managing the printing environment. Individual companies might assign this person other network administration tasks as well. The CNA is usually a full-time employee of the company and is often required to perform other duties besides managing the network.

The CNA certification provides a current or prospective employer assurance that you have a good understanding of the Novell operating system. It also certifies that you have a knowledge of the different administration tools and the different aspects of managing a network.

After becoming a CNA, the knowledge and information that you acquire can assist you in becoming a Certified NetWare Engineer (CNE). Unfortunately, the CNA test does not count towards the CNE certification. The CNA certification requires that you know the basic and advanced concepts of the Novell operating system, along with more than a basic understanding of microcomputers.

One of the first decisions you must make before pursuing the CNA certification is to decide which operating system you want to work with. Novell offers three operating systems: NetWare 2.2, NetWare 3.11 , or NetWare 4.0 . The 2.2 system is the operating system based on the Intel 286 microprocessor. This operating system is basically a modification of the 2.15 operating system that was one of Novell's biggest selling operating systems. The second choice is the 3.11 operating system. This system is a completely different operating system kernel than that of the 2.2. Although 3.11 is a completely different kernel, Novell has made the look and feel of it the same as past versions of NetWare. The third choice is the 4.0 operating system. This is Novell's latest version of the operating system.

The decision of which operating system to choose depends on which type of system you have in your office or which system you have the most experience with. As with any of the different certifications that Novell offers, the more hands-on experience you have in the subject, the better your chances of passing the exams.

The criteria for getting the CNA certification involves passing one competency exam. The exam covers the system manager and advanced system manager for either 2.2, 3.11, or 4.0. There are no questions on the exam about DOS/microcomputer concepts.

This is Novell's certification for people who are more than system administrators. Many of the people that obtain the Certified NetWare Engineer (CNE) certification are consultants, system integrators, or employees of a company that needs a person with more skill and knowledge to help maintain the overall network.

CNE responsibilities include managing the network in day-to-day activities, repairing and upgrading the hardware at both the workstations and file server, troubleshooting problems on the network, and fine-tuning the network for maximum performance. In general the overall job of the CNE is to make sure that the network stays up and running.

To obtain a CNE certification, you should have a good general understanding of microcomputers and how they work, as well as an intermediate knowledge of DOS. Other areas that you should be very familiar with are the NetWare operating system, network hardware, network cabling, and network diagnostic and troubleshooting tools.

To get certified as a CNE you must pass seven competency exams and submit an application to Novell. The exams are broken into four categories: core exams, operating system exams, CNE elective exams, and additional elective exams. The core exams consist of DOS/microcomputer concepts, NetWare service and support, and networking technologies. These required exams will give you a total of 10 credits. The next category is the operating system. This area contains the system manager and advanced system manager exams for NetWare 2.2, 3.11, and 4.0. The system manager exam is worth 3 credits and the advanced system manager exam is worth 2 credits; a total of 5 credits are needed. You can select the operating system you want to specialize in. The CNE elective exams require 4 credits. The choices are

- NetWare 2.2 System Manager (3 credits),
- NetWare 2.2 Advanced System Manager (2 credits),
- NetWare 2.15 to 2.2 Update (2 credits),
- NetWare 3.11 System Manager (3 credits),
- Netware 3.11 Advanced System Manager (2 credits),
- NetWare 3.11 OS Features Review (2 credits),
- NetWare 4.0 System Administration (3 credits),
- NetWare 4.0 Advanced Administration (2 credits), and
- Netware 3.11 to 4.0 Update (2 credits).

Additional electives include

- Product Information for Authorized Resellers (2 credits),
- Product Information for Gold Authorized Resellers (2 credits),
- LAN WorkPlace for DOS (2 credits),
- NetWare TCP/IP (2 credits),

- NetWare NFS (2 credits),
- NetWare for Macintosh Connectivity (2 credits),
- LANalyzer Basics (2 credits),
- Advanced LANalyzer for Ethernet (3 credits),
- LANtern Services Manager (2 credits),
- Advanced LANalyzer for Token Ring (3 credits),
- NetWare Dial-in/Dial-out Connectivity (2 credits), and
- NetWare for SAA Installation and Troubleshooting (3 credits).

If you select the 3.11 system manager and 3.11 advanced system manager as your operating system specialty, you cannot select any of the 3.11 system management or 3.11 OS features review exams to fulfill the four elective requirements. You can, however, choose the 2.2 or 4.0 exams to complete the 4 credits.

Novell places a time limit on getting all the CNE exam credits required for certification. From the time you take the first exam, you have one year to complete all other requirements. If in the process of certifying, Novell changes the requirements or adds additional requirements, you must follow the new certification requirements.

Once you become a CNE, you are required to maintain your certification by taking additional courses and/or exams. This usually happens if Novell releases a new or updated product or feels that CNEs should know about significant technology changes concerning networking. If continuing certification requirements are imposed, Novell will notify you by mail. After being notified of the continuing requirements, you have six months to pass the proficiency exams. If you let your CNE certification expire by not following up on the continuing certification requirements, you will have to start the certification process from the beginning to become a CNE again.

What is an ECNE?

This certification is a continuation of the CNE program. A person that becomes an Enterprise Certified NetWare Engineer (ECNE) usually has some special requirements or interests in the advanced or specialized areas of networking. An example of this is a consultant or a network administrator that needs to connect NetWare and UNIX using TCP/IP and NFS, or create a wide area network using Novell's Dial-in/Dial-out products. Other examples include NetWare SAA or NetWare for Macintosh.

ECNE responsibilities include managing the network in day-to-day activities, repairing and upgrading the hardware at both the workstations and file server, troubleshooting problems on the network, and fine-tuning the network for maximum performance. Along with these responsibilities, the ECNE must also install, maintain, and support the products and services that correspond to their ECNE specialty.

To become an ECNE you must first become certified as a CNE. You must also pass the 3.11 system manager and 3.11 advanced system manager exams. If you passed these exams en route to becoming a CNE you do not have to retake the exams. After completing the CNE and 3.11 operating system requirements, you are then required to obtain an additional 14 credits. These 14 credits can include 2.2 system management and 2.2 advanced system management, 4.0 system management and 4.0 advanced system management, or any of the other elective credits. There is no time limit imposed on getting the 14 credits. Every additional exam you take counts towards your ECNE certification.

Once you become an ECNE, Novell requires you to remain abreast of changes and enhancements in networking technology. All ECNEs are required to fulfill any continuing certification requirements offered by Novell. If Novell introduces a new or updated product, Novell might require that you demonstrate your proficiency with the product or technology by passing the related exam. Novell notifies you by mail of any new exams you must take to maintain your certification. As with the CNE certification, you have six months to complete the requirements.

What is a CNI?

This certification is for the individual who wants to teach certified NetWare courses. These courses are taught at Novell Authorized Education Centers (NAECs) and the classes must use the Novell courseware. There are two basic types of Certified NetWare Instructors (CNIs): NAEC-employed CNIs and independent CNIs. The NAEC-employed CNIs are employed full- or part-time by the NAEC and teach exclusively for that education center. Often these CNIs are required to perform other tasks besides teaching. Such duties include installing systems, acting as technical support for other employees or customers, maintaining the computer network at the NAEC, repairing and maintaining the equipment in the classroom, and teaching other non-Novell courses such as applications.

The independent CNI is normally not connected with any NAEC on an employee basis. They are usually self-employed or an employee of a consulting firm that hires out the services of the CNI. Independent CNIs are contracted by NAECs on a class-by-class need. While many NAECs employ full- or part-time CNIs to teach the scheduled classes, there are times when classes are added to the schedule and the NAEC does not employ enough CNIs to cover the added courses. NAECs also contract with independent CNIs at times to cover classes when the employed instructor becomes ill or to cover classes when the instructors are on vacation. Other NAECs do not employ any CNIs, they only contract to independents. This eliminates the overhead cost of an employee and allows the NAEC to teach classes only when profitable.

The responsibilities of the CNI vary greatly in scope. The basic responsibility is to present the Novell courseware in a professional and understandable format. The CNI must make sure that the classroom is properly set up and all hardware and software needed to conduct the class is in functioning order. Besides these responsibilities, the CNI must remain current on their certifications and keep up with changing technologies that might impact the course subject. Other responsibilities can include any other jobs or tasks that the company feels the CNI should perform.

There are three levels or categories of CNIs: category I (cat. I), category II (cat. II), and specialty CNI. The category I instructor is certified to teach the Product Information Course (PIC), NetWare 2.2 System Manager, NetWare 2.2 Advanced System Manager, NetWare 3.11 System Manager, NetWare 3.11 OS Features Review, NetWare 3.11 to 4.0 Update, and NetWare 4.0 System Administrator courses. Category II instructors are certified to teach Service and Support, Network Technologies, NetWare 3.11 Advanced System Manager, NetWare 4.0 Advanced Administration, and NetWare 4.0 Installation Workshop. The Specialty Instructor can only teach the specialty courses that they are certified in. These courses can include NetWare TCP/IP, NetWare NFS, and NetWare Dial-in/Dial-out Connectivity.

To become certified as a CNI you must first realize that it requires more time and training than the CNE or ECNE programs. To start the certification process you must first submit an application to the Area Education Manager (AEM). The applicant also needs to convince a Novell Authorized Education Center to sponsor him/her. The AEM then submits the application to Novell for approval. Once the CNI candidate is approved, they must pass the following exams designed for CNIs:

- DOS/Microcomputer Hardware Combined Exam,
- Product Information Course Exam,
- NetWare 2.2 System Manager Exam,
- NetWare 2.2 Advanced System Manager Exam, and
- NetWare 3.11 System Manager Exam.

Optional exams include

- NetWare 3.11 OS Features Review Exam,
- NetWare 3.11 to 4.0 Update Exam, and
- NetWare 4.0 System Administration Exam.

The optional exams allow the CNI to teach that class. If you want to teach all of the courses you must pass all of the listed exams.

The CNI candidate must also attend a certified class for each of the listed courses. These courses must be led by a CNI and the courses must be conducted at an NAEC. The candidate must then mail or fax a copy of each certificate they receive to Novell CNI administration.

The candidate will then be eligible to attend Novell's Train the Trainer (TTT) class. The TTT course is one week long and is held at a Novell office. The class is designed to teach the CNI how to present the material in a logical format, how to use linking, picturing, and chunking to help convey the information, how to use visual aids, and instructs the CNI in developing course lesson plans. During this course the CNI candidate leads mini-lectures from different chapters in the NetWare manuals. They are also videotaped so that they can see and critique their style.

Once the trainee passes the TTT course, the candidate becomes a Certified NetWare Instructor for the category I courses.

To become a category II instructor, the candidate must first complete the category I requirements. Once this requirement is satisfied, the candidate must pass the category II exams and attend each of the category II courses, then mail or fax a copy of the certificate to Novell CNI administration. Category II courses and exams include

- NetWare Service and Support,
- Networking Technologies,
- NetWare 3.11 Advanced System Manager,
- NetWare 4.0 Advanced Administration, and
- NetWare 4.0 Installation Workshop.

Upon meeting these requirements, the candidate must attend a one-week TTT course in which the candidate must demonstrate technical expertise and lead lab exercises from the courses. After the successful completion of all requirements, the candidate will be approved to teach category II courses.

The last area of certification for CNIs is the specialized courses. You do not have to be a category I or II instructor to become certified as a specialty instructor. The only courses you can teach are the ones you have specialized in.

The process of becoming a specialized instructor is basically the same as for the category I and II CNIs. First the candidate must obtain approval from the AEM, pass the Networking Technologies exam, attend the student course associated with the specialized topic, mail or fax a copy of the certificate to Novell CNI administration, pass the exam for the course, and attend an Instructor Evaluation Course related to the specialized course.

The following is a list of the specialized courses:

- NetWare Asynchronous Connectivity,
- NetWare for SAA,
- LANalyzer Basics,
- LANalyzer for Ethernet,
- LANalyzer for Token Ring,
- LANtern Services Manager,
- NetWare TCP/IP,
- NetWare NFS
- Programming with Btrieve,
- Programming with Btrieve: Advanced Features,
- Xtrieve Plus,
- Programming with XQL, and
- Programming with NetWare Communication Services.

As other services and products are offered, Novell will add education courses to the list of category I, II, and specialty instructor certifications.

The CNI certification is an ongoing process; the CNI must continue to stay current with each new course that is added to the category they are certified for. The CNI must also pay a yearly registration fee that covers, among other things, updates on courseware.

Creating a certification checklist

Now that you have a basic idea of what each certification entails, you can create a checklist. This checklist will help you organize your thoughts and actions to help safeguard against missing or forgetting any of the requirements. Many times when you pursue a goal or certification you begin to lose sight of what it is that you really want to accomplish and why. The use of the checklist along with an understanding of why you want or need the certification (to be covered in-depth in chapter 2) will help you maintain the proper focus to succeed.

The checklist that you create should have information about the certification you are pursuing, as well as courses and related exams. This includes dates of training courses, course numbers, dates of exams, and exam numbers. Other pieces of information in the checklist include telephone numbers of your contacts at Novell, the Novell Authorized Education Center (NAEC) facility where you attend classes, the Drake registration office, and the Drake testing office. You might also want to include the addresses of the above mentioned locations, an area for reference material, and an area for any notes.

There are two very important contacts mentioned in the previous paragraph. First, the NAEC is a training center that provides Novell certified training. The difference between someone who teaches Novell and an NAEC is much like the difference between a nonaccredited and an accredited college or university. You might learn something from either source of information, but people tend to view your credentials with less enthusiasm if you don't use an NAEC. In fact, some people will disregard your Novell training altogether if you don't receive your training from an NAEC. The reason is obvious; you receive training from a known good source if you use an NAEC. The level of training is dubious at best from any other source.

The second contact is the Drake testing center. Drake is a company that provides testing for a wide range of certifications; everyone from CPAs to registered nurses goes to Drake to take their exams. The person sitting next to you during an exam might not even know very much about computers; they might fly planes for a living. Drake testing centers appear in a wide variety of locations. You can find them in dedicated test centers or borrowing space at a training facility like a college or university. In fact, you might even find one at your local NAEC.

The Drake testing center always uses someone who is certified by them to administer the examinations you take. This person makes certain that you do not have an opportunity to cheat on the examination. They also make sure that you have any required testing materials and that your test environment is as quiet and comfortable as possible. You are required to follow any instructions they might provide and they are the only person you can talk to during the examination.

One thing that these test center administrators do not do is handle your examination. Drake downloads the examinations from the test center on a daily basis and sends them to the appropriate places. A computer automatically grades the examinations after you take them. As you can see, your examination is untouched by any human hands but your own. If you fail, there is little chance you will convince anyone that there was any problem, except a lack of study on your part. If you do notice a flaw in your examination, make sure you point it out to the test center administrator immediately. They can provide feedback to Novell and might help you out if you narrowly missed passing your examination. Reporting a problem also reduces the risk of someone else stumbling over the same problem. You should also report any problems to your contact at Novell.

Now that you understand what you want to do and who you need to contact, it's time to start a checklist. The following sample checklists will give you an idea of what you might want to include in your checklist. If you decide to use the checklists in this book, use a highlighter to mark which courses and exams you need to obtain your required credits. Be sure to add in any information that will help you reach your goals.

The checklist for the CNA certification usually is not as detailed as the ones for the CNE and ECNE certifications. The example in FIG. 1-1 lists the basic information.

Item Description		Date
Understand the responsibility of a CNA		_____
Complete goals worksheet		_____

Exam Description	Exam Number	Exam Pass Date
Certified NetWare 2.2 Administrator	50-115	_____
Certified NetWare 3.11 Administrator	50-116	_____
Certified NetWare 4.0 Administrator		_____

Other Information:

Phone numbers: _____

Dates of exams: _____

_____

Location of test center: _____

Date paperwork sent to Novell: _____

Reference materials: (books, software, etc.): _____

_____

Misc.: _____

_____

_____

1-1
Sample CNA certification checklist.

Notice that the first two items tell you when you understand the responsibility of a CNA and when you complete the goals worksheet. This is the preplanning section, knowing what and why you are doing this. The second area defines the exam description, exam date, and exam pass date. This is what you need to do to fulfill the requirements of CNA certification. As you pass the exams, fill in the dates. In the last section of the checklist, a space is provided for information such as the phone numbers of the testing center and Novell. The form includes other areas for dates of exams and the location of the test center. When filling in the test center location, make sure you include street address, cross streets, and any special directions about how to get to the test center. The next line documents when you sent your paperwork to Novell. Also provided is space for any references that might help you study or prepare for the exams and a space for any other comments or ideas you might find important. Filling out each area of the checklist ensures that you complete each step necessary to become certified.

The CNE and ECNE checklists are a little more involved than the CNA checklist. Both certifications have a list of required and elective credits that you must keep track of. Notice that this form contains additional information designed to keep you on the right path. For example, in addition to the preplanning section, we include all of the required and elective requirements. This allows you to see all of the possible selections in one place. A sample CNE checklist is shown in FIG. 1-2.

The information contained in this checklist documents preplanning responsibilities and goals, as well as the certification courses and exams. The checklist is divided into areas that help you know which areas are required and which are electives. We also added the course/exam name along with the corresponding numbers for easy reference. A note area allows you to keep track of any notes or comments you might want to make about the subject. At the end of the checklist is a section for phone numbers, addresses, contact names, and reference material. We even supplied some space for any additional information that might assist you in your quest.

The ECNE checklist in FIG. 1-3 basically follows the CNE checklist with just a few changes at the beginning of the list. Included in these changes is an area to be filled out after completing the CNE certification. The other area that has been modified has to do with keeping track of the 3.11 and 4.0 operating system requirements.

We have provided you with some ideas for creating your own checklist. Table 1-1 provides you with a reference list of all the courses and exams that Novell offers. Courses and exams are being added and removed as technology and products evolve. To find the latest course and exam offerings use the FaxBack number or the education number located in appendix A. The list includes course name and number, exam number, and credit value. We provided space at the end of the list to allow you room for course and exam additions.

Item Description	Date
Understand the responsibility of a CNE	_____
Complete goals worksheet	_____

Mandatory Core Requirements	Course Number	Course Date	Exam Number	Exam Pass Date	Credits
DOS/Microcomputer Concepts	1100-1	_____	50-15	_____	2
NetWare Service and Support	701	_____	50-46	_____	5
NetWorking Technologies	200	_____	50-80	_____	3

Operating System (5 credits required)	Course Number	Course Date	Exam Number	Exam Pass Date	Credits
NetWare 2.2 Track					
2.2 System Manager	501	_____	50-20	_____	3
2.2 Advanced System Manager	502	_____	50-44	_____	2
NetWare 3.11 Track					
System Manager	505	_____	50-91	_____	3
Advanced System Manager	515	_____	50-82	_____	2
NetWare 4.0 Track					
4.0 System Administration	520	_____	50-122	_____	3
4.0 Advanced System Administration	525	_____	50-82	_____	2
Elective Credits					
2.2 System Manager	501	_____	50-20	_____	3
2.2 Advanced System Manager	502	_____	50-44	_____	2
NetWare 2.15 to 2.2 Update	1115	_____	50-37	_____	2
3.11 System Manager	505	_____	50-91	_____	3
3.11 Advanced System Manager	515	_____	50-82	_____	2
NetWare 3.11 OS Features Review	506	_____	50-42	_____	2
NetWare 4.0 System Administration	520	_____	50-122	_____	3
4.0 Advanced System Administration	525	_____	50-123	_____	2
NetWare 3.11 to 4.0 Update	526	_____	50-124	_____	2

Note: The 2.2 elective credits and the 2.15 to 2.2 Update credits will not count as elective credits if the 2.2 track was selected as the operating system credits.

The 3.11 elective credits and the 3.11 OS Features Review credits will not count as elective credits if the 3.11 track was selected as the operating system credits.

Elective Credits (continued)

Course		Number		Exam		Credits
Product Information for Authorized Resellers	304	_____	50-18	_____	2
Product Information for Gold Authorized Resellers	305	_____	50-19	_____	2
NetWare 4.0 Design and Implementation	530	_____	50-125	_____	3
LAN WorkPlace for DOS Administration	601	_____	50-95	_____	2
NetWare TCP/IP Transport	605	_____	50-86	_____	2
NetWare NFS	610	_____	50-87	_____	2
NetWare for Macintosh Connectivity	615	_____	50-93	_____	2
LANtern Services Manager	708	_____	50-89	_____	3
NetWare Dial-in/Dial-out Connectivity	715	_____	50-112	_____	2
NetWare for SAA	720	_____	50-85	_____	3
NetWare Management System for Windows	730	_____	50-128	_____	2
NetWare 4.0 Installation Workshop	804	_____	50-126	_____	2
Btrieve: An Overview	904	_____	50-127	_____	1
LANalyzer Basics	703	_____	50-110	_____	2
Advanced LANalyzer for Ethernet	703	_____	50-111	_____	3
Advanced LANalyzer for Token Ring	711	_____	50-97	_____	3

Note: As of May 15, 1993, Novell will not offer the LANalyzer courses 703, 704, and 711. Any CNE or ECNE candidate having passed the exam can still apply the credits to their certification.[a]

NAEC/Course Information:

NAEC name: _____

Phone number: _____

Contact name: _____

Location: _____

Course start times: _____

Comments: _____

_____

Testing Information:

Phone number: _____

Dates of exams: _____

_____

Location of test center: _____

1-2 *Continued.*

Novell Information:

Date called Novell to order CNE application: _____

Date paperwork and picture sent to Novell: _____

Reference materials (books, software, etc.): _____

_____

Other: _____

_____

[a]On February 9, 1993, Novell exclusively transferred all licensing on technology of its hardware - based LANalyzer product to Network Communications Corp. (NCC). At this time Novell and NCC have agreed that this will not have an impact on the certifications of CNEs or ECNEs.

Item Description	Date
Understand the responsibility of an ECNE	_____
Complete goals worksheet	_____
CNE certification completion	_____

Operating System (3.11 and 4.0 credits required)	Course Number	Course Date	Exam Number	Exam Pass Date	Credits
NetWare 3.11 Track					
3.11 System Manager	505	_____	50-91	_____	3
3.11 Advanced System Manager	515	_____	50-82	_____	2
NetWare 4.0 Track					
4.0 System Administration	520	_____	50-122	_____	3
4.0 Advanced System Administration	525	_____	50-123	_____	2

Note: NetWare 3.11 and 4.0 are required for ECNE certification. If you select the 3.11 track, you can elect to take NetWare 3.11 to 4.0 Update or 4.0 Administration and 4.0 Advanced Administration. If you elect to take the 4.0, track you can take 3.11 OS Features Review or 3.11 System Manager and 3.11 Advanced System Manager.

Operating system and electives must total 19 credits.

1-3 *Sample ECNE certification checklist.*

Elective Credits	Course Number	Course Date	Exam Number	Exam Pass Date	Credits
2.2 System Manager	501	_____	50-20	_____	3
2.2 Advanced System Manager	502	_____	50-44	_____	2
NetWare 2.15 to 2.2 Update	1115	_____	50-37	_____	2
3.11 System Manager	505	_____	50-91	_____	3
3.11 Advanced System Manager	515	_____	50-82	_____	2
NetWare 3.11 OS Features Review	506	_____	50-42	_____	2
NetWare 4.0 System Administration	520	_____	50-122	_____	3
4.0 Advanced System Administration	525	_____	50-123	_____	2
NetWare 3.11 to 4.0 Update	526	_____	50-124	_____	2

Note: The 2.2 elective credits and the 2.15 to 2.2 Update credits will not count as elective credits if the 2.2 track was selected as the operating system credits.

The 3.11 elective credits and the 3.11 OS Features Review credits will not count as elective credits if the 3.11 track was selected as the operating system credits.

Product Information for Authorized Resellers	304	_____	50-18	_____	2
Product Information for Gold Authorized Resellers	305	_____	50-19	_____	2
NetWare 4.0 Design and Implementation	530	_____	50-125	_____	3
LAN WorkPlace for DOS Administration	601	_____	50-95	_____	2
NetWare TCP/IP Transport	605	_____	50-86	_____	2
NetWare NFS	610	_____	50-87	_____	2
NetWare for Macintosh Connectivity	615	_____	50-93	_____	2
LANtern Services Manager	708	_____	50-89	_____	3
NetWare Dial-in/Dial-out Connectivity	715	_____	50-112	_____	2
NetWare for SAA	720	_____	50-85	_____	3
NetWare Management System for Windows	730	_____	50-128	_____	2
NetWarc 4.0 Installation Workshop	804	_____	50-126	_____	2
Btrieve: An Overview	904	_____	50-127	_____	1
LANalyzer Basics	703	_____	50-110	_____	2
Advanced LANalyzer for Ethernet	703	_____	50-111	_____	3
Advanced LANalyzer for Token Ring	711	_____	50-97	_____	3

Note: As of May 15, 1993, Novell will not offer the LANalyzer courses 703, 704, and 711. Any CNE or ECNE candidate having passed the exam can still apply the credits to their certification.[a]

1-3 *Continued.*

NAEC/course information:

NAEC name: _____

Phone number: _____

Contact name: _____

Location: _____

Course start times: _____

Comments: _____

_____

Testing Information:

Phone number: _____

Dates of exams: _____

_____

Location of test center: _____

Novell Information:

Date called Novell to order CNE application: _____

Date paperwork and picture sent to Novell: _____

Reference materials (books, software, etc.): _____

_____

Other: _____

_____

_____

[a]On February 9, 1993, Novell exclusively transferred all licensing on technology of its hardware-based LANalyzer product to Network Communications Corp. (NCC). At this time Novell and NCC have agreed that this will not have an impact on the certifications of the CNEs or ECNEs.

Table 1-1 Course and exam list.

Course title	Course number	Course length	CNE/ECNE exam number	CNI exam number	Credits
Networking Technologies	200	3 days	50-80	50-81	3
Product Information for Authorized Resellers	304	2 days	50-18	50-25	2
Product Information for Authorized Gold Resellers	305	3 days	50-19	50-25	2
NetWare 2.2 System Manager	501	3 days	50-20	50-39	3
NetWare 2.2 Advanced System Manager	502	2 days	50-44	50-40	2
NetWare 3.11 System Manager	505	3 days	50-91	50-47	3
NetWare 3.11 OS Features Review	506	2 days	50-45	50-92	2
NetWare 3.11 Advanced System Manager	515	3 days	50-82	50-83	2
NetWare 4.0 Administrator	520	3 days	50-122	—	3
NetWare 4.0 Advanced Administrator	525	3 days	50-123	—	2
NetWare 3.11 to 4.0 Update	526	3 days	50-124	—	2
NetWare 4.0 Design and Implementation	530	3 days	50-125	—	3
LAN WorkPlace for DOS Administration	601	2 days	50-95	50-96	2
NetWare TCP/IP Transport	605	2 days	50-86	50-32	2
NetWare NFS	610	2 days	50-87	50-33	2
NetWare for Macintosh Connectivity	615	2 days	50-93	50-94	2
NetWare Service and Support	701	5 days	50-46	50-50	5
LANtern Services Manager	708	3 days	50-89	50-48	3
NetWare Dial-in/Dial-out Connectivity	715	2 days	50-112	50-212	2
NetWare for SAA Installation and Troubleshooting	720	3 days	50-85	50-30	3
NetWare Management System for Windows	730	2 days	50-128	50-228	3
NetWare 4.0 Installation Workshop	804	2 days	50-126	—	2
Btrieve: An Overview	904	1 day	50-127	50-227	1
Programming with Btrieve	905	3 days	50-12	50-13	3
Programming with Btrieve Advanced Features	906	—	50-14	50-41	3
Xtrieve PLUS	907	2 days	—	50-210	2
Programming with XQL	910	—	50-16	50-17	3
Programming with NetWare Communication Service	920	—	50-42	50-43	2
Developing NetWare Loadable Modules (NLMs)	930	3 days	—	50-213	1

Conclusion As you have seen in this chapter, the CNA, CNE, ECNE, and CNI certification process takes some planning. It takes more than just calling Novell and asking for an application. You must know which certification best emphasizes your knowledge and expertise. By knowing what the responsibilities and requirements include, you are better prepared for a successful certification completion.

The procedure for becoming certified might seem difficult if you do not preplan adequately. As you have seen in this chapter the list of exams is quite long and there are many different ways to put together a certification program. By first deciding which certification you will seek and using the corresponding checklist, you can then decide which areas you want to pursue. After selecting the correct checklist you can highlight the appropriate exams and start filling in the missing data.

You now have the basic requirements and duties of the Novell certified professional. The ground work you do now will greatly enhance your chances of becoming certified. Before you continue into chapter 2, take some time to examine your skills, knowledge, and what direction you want to take. Then fill out the checklist; this will give you the path and goal for success.

2 *Understanding the certification process*

The first chapter provided you with a better understanding of what each certification will help you accomplish. However, this is the company view of the certification. It only answers part of the question, "What can the certification do for my current company?" This is great for your employer, but it doesn't help you understand how to accomplish this feat or why you should even attempt it. Everyone wants more from an educational experience than to simply fulfill a company requirement. Fortunately, Novell certification can help you in a more personal way. It can pave the way to new jobs with higher pay and more interesting work. Instead of helping the boss juggle paperwork all day, with the right certification you can run your own department in a larger company. Even if you're self-employed, a certification can help you increase your clientele and allow you to charge a higher hourly rate. In many cases a certification provides the basis for starting your own networking business.

This chapter helps you concentrate on how a certification helps you. It answers questions like, "Why is certification important?" and "How do I obtain my personal goals as well as the company's goals?" Once you understand these concepts, you can take a detailed look at the certification requirements. This will help you complete the certification checklist you started in chapter 1.

Introduction

This chapter also helps you in scheduling the time required to complete a certification. Believe it or not, the major reason many people fail to get certified is a lack of time. Certification requires a personal investment just like any other educational experience. You must schedule time to take classes, study, and take exams. What is more important, you must schedule time for continuing education. Many people attend classes, but cut a few because they don't quite have the time required to attend. Then they try to take the exams without studying. Finally, because they are totally unprepared to take the exams, they get frustrated after the first few questions and rush through the rest. This is a sure way to fail. Even the people who do get certified can lose their certification if they don't attend to continuing education requirements. Certification, more than anything else, means that you are willing to devote the time required to maintain a specific level of education and competency. The guidelines in this chapter help you schedule that time.

Why do you need certification?

There are many people who look at certification as simply another "sheepskin" to hang on the wall. Certification is a lot more than some classroom study and a few exams. It is a commitment by you to maintain a specific level of training in order to perform a set of very specific tasks. It also involves the personal satisfaction of knowing that you have the skills to perform a job to the standards set by the industry.

Discovering exactly what certification will do for you is a big part of completing the requirements successfully. You need to keep these goals in mind as you choose classes and prepare for exams. Having a goal also helps when you take exams and set aside time to maintain your proficiency. Figure 2-1 provides you with some ideas of how to create your own goals worksheet. You can use this worksheet to help you throughout the certification process.

As you can see, the form is very straightforward. It contains blanks for your name, the certification you intend to pursue, and the date you plan to obtain it. Make sure you keep both the Certification and Anticipated date of completion fields up-to-date as you progress. Explanations of the Goals area fields appear in the following paragraphs. You should couple this form with the Certification Checklist found in chapter 1.

The following paragraphs examine the reasons for certification in detail. Make sure you list the reasons that fit your situation on your Goals Worksheet. Listing the reasons you are doing something at the beginning of a project often helps you complete it. These reasons help you to focus on the goals you set at the start of the certification process and emphasize the personal need to complete it.

Name: _____

Certification: _____

Anticipated date of completion: _____

Goals:

Professional recognition: _____

_____

_____

_____

Network skills: _____

_____

_____

_____

Industry trend: _____

_____

_____

_____

Novell support: _____

_____

_____

_____

_____

Other: _____

_____

_____

_____

2-1
*Novell certification
goals checklist.*

There are many people stuck in "dead end" jobs that would prefer to do something else. Many administrative assistants or other semiskilled personnel would prefer a job with a little excitement, rather than the same old work every day. A Novell certification can help you reach that goal. Even if you do have a fairly interesting job, a Novell certification can provide the variety that makes work interesting. Instead of spending all day every day shuffling papers, you could spend part of that time working with a network.

***Professional
recognition***

Another group of people who really need Novell certification to gain professional recognition are consultants. How many times has a client asked why they should use you rather than Joe or Mary down the street? Have you had to lower your per hour charge just to get a job? Wouldn't it be nice to have a reason that you could show in no uncertain terms to the client? These are all reasons why a consultant would want professional recognition; not only to increase self-satisfaction and gain a reputation among your peers, but to gain the respect of your clients as well.

As you can see, professional recognition goes a long way toward making every day an adventure rather than an exercise in boredom. A Novell certification is a good way of getting the professional recognition you need to attain this goal. Of course, these are only two ways that professional recognition can help. Now it is time for you to think about how professional recognition will help you. Make sure you write it down on your Goals Worksheet.

Network skills Network skills is one area that you might not feel concerns you. Perhaps you have had some hands-on experience with a network before and you keep up with the latest news in the trade journals. No matter what you think your level of experience is, certification training is always the best method for gaining network skills.

While on-the-job training is a viable way of gaining some information, it does not give you all the advantages of certification training. When you go through network classes, the instructor provides you with information based on the input of hundreds or even thousands of other people. There is no way to gain this type of information in the vacuum of on-the-job training. Even if you could gain the book knowledge, certification training provides you with at least one other valuable asset. You get to test this input in a laboratory environment. Your company won't let you test the knowledge you gain on the company LAN, but you can test it at a training center. This ensures that you really know how specific networking conditions look and how to fully install all the features of the Novell NetWare operating system.

Skills include both knowledge from books and practical experience from hands-on training. You will likely spend as much time using your new skills as you will learning them. The instructor is there to help you fully comprehend what the manuals contain. How often have you read the manuals, only to feel like you didn't know any more when you finished than when you started? In many cases you understand what the manuals say, but fail to implement the procedures correctly. Learning from an instructor through certification training gives you the feeling of knowing NetWare, not simply taking your best guess about what you think will happen.

Because every trainee begins with a different level of knowledge, it is important that you gauge what you know with what you expect to learn. This is one of the goals that will help you keep on track. Once you determine what you expect to gain from the certification process regarding network skills, then you need to write it down. Keep this goal in mind as you take each of your courses. Also use it as a guide for helping you study. Concentrate on your weak areas before taking the exam.

A weak but viable reason to get certified is that it is an industry trend. Many companies do not want to trust the valuable information on their network to someone who doesn't possess the proper training. References are nice, but a certificate is just as good in many cases. Having a CNA, CNE, ECNE, or CNI certificate will open many employment opportunities for you. Of course, having both experience and a certification is almost a sure winner at the negotiation table. As you can see, having the proper credentials always works to your benefit.

Industry trends

This is probably a good time for you to write down some of the ways you can use your certification once you get it. Make sure you look at the various trade papers that show how industry trends will help you in gaining the type of employment you want. You can write these trends down or even take clippings from the trade papers to use for future reference.

Clippings from trade magazines and newspapers are especially important for consultants. They provide an extra level of credibility when you bid on a large networking job. Remember that the client is more apt to listen to what the industry has to say than to simply take your word that certification is a good and necessary requirement when finding someone to install a network.

Novell provides an added layer of support for people who are certified to use their products. After all, it only makes good business sense for them to do so. There are several mechanisms that Novell uses to accomplish this.

Novell support

- Special assistance on the Novell product support line.
- A forum on CompuServe where you can discuss new advances in networking technology or get a little help with an especially thorny problem. You can also use this forum to download new versions of drivers and programs.
- Use of the Novell logo for your price sheets, advertising pamphlets, business cards, and resume. Only a certified person may use this logo.
- One year's free subscription to the Network Support Encyclopedia; a software library crammed with information about Novell products. It also contains articles and papers describing how to overcome specific networking problems.

As you can see, Novell's commitment to the certificate holder is just as great as the commitment you must have to get certified. The ability to receive special support from a company also works to both an employer's and a client's benefit. If these people know that you can provide them with better-than-average support because of your relationship with Novell, it could work to your advantage in getting a job. You need to keep this support in mind when selling your skills to a potential employer or client.

Other reasons   By now your head is buzzing with other ideas about how certification can help you. Make sure you write them down while they are fresh in your mind. These ideas could prove to be the difference between failing and passing as time progresses. In addition, personalizing your goals list might provide the edge you need to gain an advantage over the competition.

What if you decide to bid on a job that another certified person has already bid on? Telling your client how your approach to networking differs from the competition can make the difference between getting the job or giving it to your competitor. You need to base part of this reasoning on how you approach your certification.

How about a job opportunity where more than one certified person has applied? Telling a potential employer how you see your certification might make them take notice. Make sure you let people know that you took the time and effort to get the most out of your valuable certification training. Give them a reason to view you as someone who is willing to put a little more effort into doing the job right.

What are the certification requirements?   Now that you have a better idea of why you want to get certified, we need to take a detailed look at how you go about it. The following paragraphs provide you with a detailed look at the certification requirements for each level of certification.

CNA   The Certified NetWare Administrator (CNA) is the lowest level certification you can obtain. The goal of this certification is to set a certain level of training for people who want to administer a specific type of NetWare LAN. There are three certificates available: NetWare 2.2 Administrator, NetWare 3.11 Administrator, and NetWare 4.0 Administrator. The requirements for this program appear in FIG. 2-2.

As you can see from FIG. 2-2, the certification process for CNA is fairly simple. Of course, the first step is to take the appropriate courses. (If you don't feel that you know enough about DOS, you will want to go to the DOS for NetWare Users and Microcomputer Concepts for NetWare Users courses as well.) Many people feel that going to these courses is unnecessary. However, even if you have previous NetWare experience, you will need to know the Novell way of maintaining a network. This is the most correct way to perform a task based on the experiences of literally thousands of other administrators.

---

1. If you don't work with DOS on a daily basis, you might want to start your study with the DOS for NetWare Users course. You will also want to take the Microcomputer Concepts for NetWare Users course. Novell will not test you on this information, but you will need it for your certification specific classes.

2. Take the appropriate courses. These include NetWare 2.2 System Manager and NetWare 2.2 Advanced System Manager for the NetWare 2.2 Adminstrator certification; NetWare 3.11 System Manager and NetWare 3.11 Advanced System Manager for the NetWare 3.11 Adminstrator certification; or NetWare 4.0 Administration and NetWare 4.0 Advanced Administration for the NetWare 4.0 Administrator certification.

3. Study the student manuals provided during the class. Make sure you study any weak areas in your knowledge skills. Check any notes you might have for information that does not appear in the manuals.

4. Schedule your exam by calling 1-800-RED-EXAM. Take the appropriate test: 50-115, Certified NetWare 2.2 Administrator; 50-116, Certified NetWare 3.11 Administrator; or 50-XXX, Certified NetWare 4.0 Administrator.

2-2
CNA certification at a glance.

5. Submit your paperwork to Novell. You can call 1-800-NETWARE to find out about the status of your paperwork. (Ask for the CNA administrator when you call.)

6. Subscribe to one or more trade journals that allow you to keep up on industry events and advances in network technology. Examples of trade journals for this level of certification include *PC Magazine* and *PC Week*. Both periodicals include network specific sections on a regular basis. If you have a specialty area, you might want to find a magazine that leans toward that specialty. For example, if you work with database management systems, you might want to get a periodical such as *Data Based Advisor* for database specific networking tips.

7. Watch your mailbox for your certification papers and any other Novell information.

The next step is to study for the exam. We recommend that you avoid cluttering your thoughts with information from too many sources. Take time to study your class notes and the student manuals thoroughly. This represents the best possible method for passing the exams. Make sure you spend extra time studying the areas you are weak in. You might even want to have someone else quiz you on various aspects of the material contained in the CNA manuals.

Once you feel you know enough about NetWare, schedule your exams. If you are a morning person, schedule the exams in the morning, likewise if you are an afternoon person. Always schedule the exams when you are most alert. Remember, you only have your brain to work with when it comes time to take the exams. There are no books allowed in the examination room. You might want to consider the day of the week as well. Some people schedule their exams on a Monday, when they feel most rushed. Don't fall into this mistake. Schedule your exams for a day when you really have time to take them.

Immediately after you complete your tests, make sure you submit your paperwork to Novell. You will probably need to call Novell from time to time to check on the progress of your paperwork. Novell also issues a picture identification card to you, so you need to provide them with a photograph. You can usually obtain a suitable picture from any passport photo store.

While you wait for your certification papers to arrive, you might want to go to your local bookstore and browse the shelves for books and periodicals that pertain to networking. Make sure you get material you can understand. It doesn't matter how well the book or periodical explains networking technology if you can't grasp what it means. B. Dalton's Software Etc. and Walden Books both provide well-stocked periodical stands. If you don't have one of these stores in your area, look for a technical bookstore. *PC Magazine* and *PC Week* both contain a wide variety of material that a network administrator needs to know. For example, they both contain product reviews along with their networking articles. Periodicals include any Novell supplied materials as well. You might want to maintain a subscription to *NetWare Connection* so you can keep abreast of the latest innovations in NetWare. (See appendix B for ideas on what trade papers you should read to find out what's going on in the networking industry.)

CNE The Certified NetWare Engineer (CNE) certification is one of the most common certifications that people get. In most cases this is the level of certification that a consultant would want. This is also the level of certification that an administrator of a large network would want.

Because this certification allows you to work with every operating system that Novell provides, it requires a lot more preparation and training than the CNA course. Of course, many of the points presented in that section are equally applicable here. Figure 2-3 provides an overview of the CNE certification process.

1. Take the appropriate courses. Chapter 1 provides a complete listing of the courses you can take. Make sure you take all the required courses and exams. You will want to spend a little time considering which elective courses to take. For example, you might want to take the NetWare for Macintosh Connectivity course if you have Macintosh computers attached to your network.

2. Study the student manuals provided during the class. Make sure you study any weak areas in your knowledge skills. Check any notes you might have for information that does not appear in the manuals. Studying one student manual at a time can help reduce your confusion level when taking the associated exam.

3. Schedule your exams by calling 1-800-RED-EXAM. Take the appropriate exams for both the required and optional courses you attended. Make sure you leave enough time between exams to allow for study. Don't rush the exams. However, you must make sure that you do take all the exams within the 12-month time frame allotted by Novell.

4. Submit your paperwork to Novell. You can call 1-800-NETWARE to find out about the status of your paperwork. (Ask for the CNE administrator when you call.)

2-3
CNE certification at a glance.

5. You probably already subscribe to one or more trade journals, such as *PC Magazine* or *PC Week*. Make sure you also subscribe to one or more network-specific trade journals that allow you to keep up on industry events and advances in network technology. Examples of trade journals for this level of certification include *LAN Times and Network World*. These magazines provide a much more intense view of networking than more generic magazines. If you have a specialty area, you might want to find a magazine that leans toward that bias. For example, if you work with database management systems, you might want to get a periodical such as *Data Based Advisor* for database specific networking tips.

6. Watch your mailbox for your certification papers and any other Novell information.

7. Check with various printers about the cost of adding your new certification sticker to your resume, price lists, or advertisements. When your certification papers arrive, make sure you add the Novell logo to show that you've completed the required certification.

As you can see from FIG. 2-3, the process for becoming a CNE is very straightforward. You go through about the same steps as a CNA does, but at a much more intense level with more courses and tests to take. While the CNA only takes one exam, the CNE must take seven. You might want to read through the explanation in the CNA section if you have any questions about the basic process for becoming a CNE.

Of course, there are other differences between the CNE and CNA certification as well. For example, you get to choose between several elective courses. This is one area where the CNE can really hone his/her skills for the environment they intend to pursue. As stated in FIG. 2-3, you could decide to pursue Macintosh connectivity as one of your electives. This is one of those areas where you must think about what you want to do with your certification before you actually begin the process. Make sure you fill out your goals worksheet (FIG. 2-1). This is an item that you could place in the Other category.

CNEs that run their own business will also want to check on the cost for placing their logo on price lists and advertisements. Even if you have to spend a little money, the recognition you receive from placing this logo on your forms will really increase business. No one will know that you went through all the training required to receive this valuable certification unless you advertise it. Make sure you get all the value you can out of the certification process.

CNEs that are going to work for a company might want to place the CNE logo on their resume. A logo of this type can really help differentiate your resume from all the others in the stack. In fact, it can make the difference between a potential employer actually reading your entire resume or tossing it after looking at the first few lines. The logo will definitely attract the attention of anyone who looks at your resume; use it to your benefit.

One final area where a CNE differs from a CNA is in the literature that you read. We assume that you already read magazines like *PC Magazine* and *PC Week*. These are the magazines that people who really want to know about the computer industry read even before they become a CNE. The magazines you need to consider subscribing to include those such as *LAN Times* and *Network World*. These magazines really cover networking in detail. They provide you with that added advantage in knowledge that you will need when talking with a client. Keeping yourself up to date on all the latest industry trends really makes a difference. For example, you might know of some new technology that works better and costs less than the old technology recommended by a competitor.

The Enterprise Certified NetWare Engineer (ECNE) certification is really an advanced form of CNE certification. It is for those people who require a little more education to perform their work. In most cases this is because they work with wide area networks (WANs) or other large network situations. As shown in FIG. 2-4, you start as a CNE before you go to this program. Chapter 1 provides you with all the details about the rights and responsibilities of this certification.

ECNE

---

1. Perform all the steps required to become a CNE (see FIG. 2-3). Once you complete this step and feel comfortable with your skills as a CNE, you can go on to complete the requirements for an ECNE.

    Note: You do not need to perform step 2 if you have already completed 3.11 System Manager and 3.11 Advanced System Manager or 4.0 Administrator and 4.0 Advanced Administrator courses in pursuit of your CNE certification.

2. Complete the 3.11 System Manager and 3.11 Advanced System Manager courses. (As an alternative, you can complete the 4.0 Administrator and 4.0 Advanced Administrator courses.) Schedule then take the 3.11 System Manager and 3.11 Advanced System Manager exams.

3. You must obtain an additional 19 credits. Novell does not place any time limit on completing this step. The only requirement for these 19 credits is that you take courses and exams that you have not taken for the CNE certification. This includes 2.2 System Management and 2.2 Advanced System Management, 4.0 System Management and 4.0 Advanced System Management, or any of the other elective credits.

    2-4
    ECNE certification at a glance.

4. Make sure you file the required paperwork after you take each exam. You can call 1-800-NETWARE to find out about the status of your paperwork. (Ask for the ECNE administrator when you call.)

5. Watch your mailbox for your certification papers and any other Novell information.

6. Check with various printers about the cost of adding your new certification sticker to your resume, price lists, or advertisements. When your certification papers arrive, make sure you add the Novell logo to show that you've completed the required certification.

Figure 2-4 shows you how to become an ECNE. Notice that you must start as a CNE and work your way through the ECNE program. The bulk of the difference between this program and the CNE program is the 19 additional credits you must obtain prior to certification.

CNI   The Certified NetWare Instructor (CNI) certification is far different than any of the other certifications that have been discussed in this chapter. To become a CNI, you must go through extra preparation and intense training. Unlike the other certifications, you *must* attend the Novell classes to become a CNI. In addition, these classes must be taught by someone certified by Novell. Figure 2-5 provides you with an overview of the requirements for this certification.

Specialty CNI and Category 1

1. Submit an application to become a CNI to the Area Education Manager (AEM). Once you complete this task, you must convince a Novell Authorized Education Center (NAEC) to sponsor you during the certification process. After you get a sponsor, the AEM will submit your application to Novell for approval.

   Note: The specialty CNI does, not have to take all the category I classes; only the class and exam that applies to the specialty.

2. Take the appropriate courses. Chapter 1 provides a complete list of the courses you can take. Unlike the other certifications, you must take the following courses and pass the associated exams: DOS/Microcomputer Hardware, Product Information, NetWare 2.2 System Manager, NetWare 2.2 Advanced System Manager, and NetWare 3.11 System Manager. Make sure you take all the required courses and exams. You will want to spend a little time considering which elective courses to take. Every optional class represents one class you can teach. Unlike the other certifications, you must take the classes to become a CNI.

2-5
CNI certification at a glance.

3. Study the student manuals provided during the class. Make sure you study any weak areas in your knowledge skills. Check any notes you might have for information that does not appear in the manuals. Studying one student manual at a time can help reduce your confusion level when taking the associated exam.

4. Schedule your exams by calling 1-800-RED-EXAM. Take the appropriate exams for both the required and optional courses you attended. Make sure you leave enough time between exams to allow for study. Don't rush the exams. However, you must make sure that you take all the exams within the 12-month time frame allotted by Novell.

5. Attend and pass Novell's Train the Trainer (TTT) class. Chapter 1 provides complete details about the requirements for this class.

6. Submit your paperwork to Novell. Make sure you include the class certifications from each class you took. You can call 1-800-NETWARE to find out about the status of your paperwork. (Ask for the CNI administrator when you call.)

7. You probably already subscribe to one or more trade journals, such as *PC Magazine* or *PC Week*. Make sure you also subscribe to one or more network specific trade journals that will allow you to keep up on industry events and advances in network technology. Examples of trade journals for this level of certification include *LAN Times* and *Network World*. These magazines provide a much more intense view of networking than more generic magazines. If you have a specialty area, you might want to find a magazine that leans toward that bias. For example, if you work with database management systems, you might want to get a periodical such as *Data Based Advisor* for the database specific networking tips.

8. Watch your mailbox for your certification papers and any other Novell information.

9. Check with various printers about the cost of adding your new certification sticker to your resume, price lists, or advertisements. When your certification papers arrive, make sure you add the Novell logo to show that you've completed the required certification.

Category II

1. Fulfill all the requirements for CNI category I. Make sure you get verification from Novell before you proceed to the next step.

2. Attend all the required category II classes listed in chapter 1.

3. Study the student manuals provided during the class. Make sure you study any weak areas in your knowledge skills. Check any notes you have for information that does not appear in the manuals. Studying one student manual at a time might help reduce your confusion level when taking the associated exam.

4. Schedule your exams by calling 1-800-RED-EXAM. Take the appropriate exams for both the required and optional courses you attended. Make sure you leave enough time between exams to allow for study. Don't rush the exams. However, you must make sure that you take all the exams within the 12-month time frame allotted by Novell.

5. Submit your paperwork to Novell. Make sure you include the class certifications from each class you took. You can call 1-800-NETWARE to find out about the status of your paperwork. (Ask for the CNI administrator when you call.)

6. Watch your mailbox for your certification papers and any other Novell information.

As you can see, there are three paths you can choose. The first two paths are for either a specialty CNI or a category I CNI certification. Review the CNI description in chapter 1 if you would like additional information on the rights and responsibilities of both these classifications. The third path is for a category II CNI certification. Notice that you must complete the requirements for category I certification before you can start the category II requirements for CNI.

This certification starts differently than the other certifications. You must first get approval to even start the process of becoming a CNI. This certification also requires you to obtain an NAEC sponsor. Unlike the other certifications, you cannot immediately start this certification process by taking classes. You must do a little preparation in advance.

Once you get past the first step, you will also need to take some special CNI examinations. Unlike the other certification programs, you must provide proof that you meet certain levels of computer competency. You need to pass both the hardware/software and the product information courses and exams besides other required courses and exams.

Like the other certification programs, there are a series of required courses and exams you can take for the CNI certification. However, because Novell requires you to take all the courses, there are no optional courses for this category of CNI certification. You can read about this procedure in the CNA section of this chapter. The most important difference to take into consideration is that you must take the courses. Novell requires proof that you passed the courses in the form of a photocopy of your certificate before it will consider you for certification.

After you complete all these certification requirements, you must attend Novell's Train the Trainer (TTT) course. Essentially this course covers the one requirement that is different between CNE/ECNE and CNI. Not only must you know how to do the work yourself, but you must teach it to others. This is the purpose behind forcing you to take the courses. You can learn by example how to teach the courses, then put this training into practice during the TTT course. You must pass this course before Novell will allow you to become a CNI.

CNIs that run their own business will also want to check on the cost of placing their logo on price lists and advertisements. Even if you have to spend a little more money, the recognition you receive from placing this logo on your forms will really increase business. In fact, no NAEC will hire you without proof of this certification. While you can continue to use your certification as a consultant installing LANs, this is not the reason you went through all that training. Make sure you make it very clear that you have all the required credentials. As you can see, the value of this certification is in actually acquiring it. You cannot teach certified Novell courses without it.

CNIs that are going to work for a company (usually an NAEC) might want to place the CNI logo on their resume. A logo of this type can really make your resume stand out from all the others in the stack. In fact, a potential employer will likely toss your resume if your certification is not immediately apparent. An NAEC will not waste time interviewing someone who is not qualified.

Category II CNIs start at the category I level as shown in FIG. 2-5. The main difference is in the amount of education and the number of exams required for category II CNI certification. Chapter 1 provides you with a complete list of these additional required classes and exams.

How long does certification take?

Some people look at the time required to gain certification as the number of hours spent in class and the time required to take exams. Nothing could be further from the truth. The certification process is ongoing and requires a commitment if you want to maintain it. There are paperwork and continuing education requirements that you must consider in addition to the more obvious requirements. The following paragraphs provide you with the information you need to take all these factors into account.

Training

The time you spend in training depends on the certification you plan to achieve. In most cases the courses are two to five days long. Chapter 1 contains a table that tells you the exact length of each class. To obtain the total time required to complete the training requirements for certification, simply add the times required for each class you intend to take.

The important consideration for this time requirement is not really the length of each class, but coordinating the class time. It helps to talk with your local NAEC representative to get a listing of course availability and dates. Simply mark out the days for each course on a calendar to plan for the time you need to spend in training.

There is another way to look at the training time investment. It is very unlikely that time will allow you to schedule more than one class per week. As a result, you can simply count the number of classes you need to take, and count it as the number of weeks you need to set aside for training. This allows you some time each week to get work done at your job or business.

Testing

As a practical rule, no one can tell you exactly how long testing will take. The problem is that while the exam times are a constant, study time is not. Taking an exam before you study for it is likely to produce very frustrating results. You need to plan sufficient study time or you will fail the exam.

A general rule of thumb that you can follow is to plan at least two hours of study per day for the same number of days it took you to complete a course. For example, if you had a four-day course, then you should plan eight hours of study time. Of course, you should not try to get all your studying done in one day. Plan for a maximum of three hours per day. Any more study time during one day reduces the effectiveness of your study time.

Make sure you include at least one hour plus travel time to take the exam itself. For example, if it takes about 20 minutes to travel from your office to the testing center, plan on at least 1 hour and 40 minutes for the exam. Remember that you need to get to the testing center at least 15 minutes early. You should add this additional time to your estimate as well.

Paperwork The time required to complete your paperwork is fairly flexible. It really depends on the availability of resources to get the required documentation together and the time required in communication with Novell. A good rule of thumb is to plan at least six hours for completing the paperwork. This includes an hour at the photographer to take your picture, at least an hour to complete the paperwork itself, about half an hour to copy the required certificates, about an hour in communication time with the testing center/NAEC, and at least two-and-one-half hours talking with a Novell representative. Of course, you will need to spend additional time getting your logo put on business forms and price lists.

Continuing education How much time is too much or too little for continuing your education? It really varies by individual requirements. You must consider what you plan to learn about, what your current level of education is, and what the requirements of your company/clients are. A good rule of thumb is at least one hour training time per day for CNEs without any special requirements, such as database management tasks. A CNA can probably get by with about half that investment, while a CNI probably requires quite a bit more. Make sure you spend enough time both reading and practicing so you feel comfortable with the level of your skills. Trying to learn at least one new item per day is probably a good idea. Make sure you spend a little time trying out new ideas with the network itself. Perhaps a different directory arrangement or a new menuing system will help improve overall system efficiency. Investing in yourself is good for both you and the company. Besides, you will never maintain your certification if you do not take the time required to train.

This chapter has provided you with information about three very important areas of certification. First, we looked at why you need to get certified. Second, we took a detailed look at the educational requirements for certification. Finally, we helped you plan the time required to get certified. When you view all three of these elements as a whole, you come up with a single plan that will help guarantee a successful certification.

Remember that certification is not merely a "sheepskin" to hang on the wall. It is much more than that. First, it proves to you and the programming community that you have the skills required to maintain a network. Self-confidence and the confidence of others are major milestones for a career in network management. Second, you can learn things in class that you will never learn on the job or from trade magazines. The major reason for this is that you have set aside time to learn about networks in a classroom environment during the certification process. Third, people who hire network professionals are increasingly aware of the benefits of using a Novell certified individual to manage their network. Finally, you get Novell's help in solving problems as part of your certification.

Make sure you understand the requirements for your particular certification program. You cannot prepare for what you do not expect. Learn about all the requirements: classroom, study, exam, paperwork, and continuing education. List everything you need to do on your checklist so that you leave nothing to chance. Preparation is an important factor in the certification process.

Time is also an important element in getting certified. Your investment does not stop after you take the classes or exams. Certification requires an investment in time even after you fulfill all the requirements. Not only is there a stack of paperwork that you must see through to completion, but there are continuing education requirements to consider as well.

3 *Learning the trade*

By this point you should have in mind the certification that best suits your experience and knowledge. It might be the CNA certification and you are using it as a stepping stone to the CNE certification, which is a stepping stone to becoming an ECNE. Maybe you have the qualifications to become a CNE already. Whatever the case, to reach the next level of certification you need to expand your understanding of the theories and practical experience of some aspect of networking.

The expansion of your experience can come in a variety of ways. It might come as on-the-job training (OJT), reading trade magazines, attending seminars or lectures, or by the hands-on trial-and-error method. Other ways to get the experience you need for advancement might come from a formal education. This formal education can come in different ways, such as attending Novell courses, vendor training from companies such as Compaq or 3Com, or obtaining a degree from a college or university. Many times an organization will prefer that you have a certification, such as the Novell CNE, before it will let you maintain its network, and if you want to advance into a higher position or into management, the company will require you to have a college degree.

In chapter 2 the requirements needed to become certified by Novell as a networking expert were covered. In this chapter we explore different ways to learn the trade. This includes the type of training that's required

Introduction

for your particular situation (or if it's necessary). If training is in your future, what level of training will you need? It is very important to get the proper level of training so you can advance your career as easily and quickly as possible. Finally, we will cover how to get the most from what you learn.

Is training really required?

Is training required? Yes. The level and amount of training depends on your situation. If you want to do more in this industry, and we assume you do or you would not have picked up this book or considered becoming certified by Novell as a networking expert, you will need more training. There is always someone claiming to be an expert, and without any training. That might be true for some areas, but there is no one that knows everything there is to know about networking (or even computers in general). The person who believes they are an expert in everything, is only fooling themselves. They are cheating themselves out of really learning, growing, and becoming all that they can be in this business.

You now have an understanding from chapter 1 of the requirements and responsibilities of the different certifications. You have also completed the goals worksheet from chapter 2, so you know exactly what certification you want to obtain and what it means to you. The certification process has been outlined as well, so you know what to expect and what you are trying to accomplish with your education. Armed with this information you can now decide if education for obtaining the certification will be required.

To decide if you need education take a look at the job duties, or if you are trying to advance in a company, look at the job description. If your education and experience meet the criteria, then you might not need any special training. If you are not totally confident in what's required for the certification or job description you are applying for, then some form of training will be necessary.

Deciding your level of training

The level of training depends on how comfortable you feel with the subject matter. You might only need a few hours of review with a student manual, or you might need to spend a few years developing the skill required to reach your goal. If your goal is to become a CNE and you now have a CNA certification or have been working with Novell NetWare for some time, chances are good that by attending the Novell courses from an NAEC and with some studying, you will pass the exams. On the other hand, if you have not had much hands-on experience with NetWare or do not know much about networking, you will have a hard time becoming certified. This is not to say that it is impossible. There are many people who have become certified by only studying the student manuals they borrowed from someone else. Unfortunately, once they get out into the workplace it becomes apparent that they are not qualified to service or administer a network. These are the people that give the certification a bad name. Luckily, these people get weeded out of the marketplace in a short time; clients and employers hear of their bad reputation and refuse to have anything to do with them. It doesn't take long for their reputation to get passed around.

To help you decide what levels of training you actually need, you need to know which certification you want and at what level your skills are. The chart in FIG. 3-1 will help you gain an understanding of your skill level. This chart along with your goals worksheet from chapter 2 will help to pinpoint your level of expertise. The key to making these worksheets and charts work is being truthful with yourself. We all want to believe that we have more expertise or knowledge than we really have. Remember, only you will see this chart. No one else needs to know how you rank yourself. When ranking yourself on the skills chart, choose the lower level of the skill ranking if you have any doubts about your skill. This will help you to strengthen any weak areas you might have and will reinforce the subject matter.

The chart can be separated into four areas. The first area lists the skills that an expert in Novell networks must know and will perform in the field. This is only a general sampling of the different skills. You might find that within a skill you know some of the subtopics very well and other subtopics need improvement. Remember, the key is to be honest with yourself. Extra space is available at the bottom of the skill list so that you can add any additional skills you think are necessary. If you are a manager and are helping your employees become certified, you will want to include any unique or special requirements specific to your company or that you feel are necessary for certification.

The second section within the chart is the ranking area. This is the section where you will rank yourself on a scale of 1 to 10. The rankings are listed from high to low, with 10 being a high ranking and 1 being a low ranking. Remember to be honest when ranking yourself; this is for your eyes only and will be a study index. If you overrate yourself, you might be missing out on studying an area you are weak in. When selecting your ranking, place a check mark under the appropriate skill level. If you feel you are between levels place the check mark to the low side of the scale.

At the bottom of the skills chart is a third section. This section has the label "Areas Needing Improvement." In this area write down the specific areas that you need to improve in. This will be both general topics from the skills section and specific subtopics from within the general skills. Be

SKILLS	LEVEL									
	High									Low
	10	9	8	7	6	5	4	3	2	1
DOS										
Microcomputer hardware										
NetWare concepts										
NetWare features										
NetWare 2.x system administration										
NetWare 3.x system administration										
NetWare 4.x system administration										
NetWare 2.x installation										
NetWare 3.x installation										
NetWare 4.x installation										
Workstation installation/setup										
Fine-tuning Netware 2.x										
Fine-tuning Netware 3.x										
Fine-tuning NetWare 4.x										
System back-up										
Printing										
Security										
User/group accounts										
Console utilities (2.x, 3.x, 4.x)										
Command line utilities (2.x, 3.x, 4.x)										
NetWare upgrading										
Topologies										

3-1 *Skill level ranking chart.*

Network technologies										
Others:										

Prepared   Areas needing improvement

_____   _____

_____   _____

_____   _____

_____   _____

_____   _____

_____   _____

_____   _____

_____   _____

specific when filling out this area, as it will be the base for study. This will help you identify what your weak points are, and then knowing what they are, you can focus on acquiring that information. If you feel you need more room to document your improvement areas, continue them on another piece of paper. Do not shortchange yourself by not including all of your improvement areas. These are your weak areas and to become not only certified but a professional networking person you must target your weak points and concentrate your efforts on these topics.

The fourth and final section can be found to the left of "Areas Needing Improvement." Fill in this section with a date when you feel you know the subject matter included in your weak areas. Keeping track of your milestones is important; it provides you with a feeling of accomplishment. By recording the date you feel comfortable with your weak points, you will feel at ease to move on to another topic.

Compare your goals worksheet and skills chart to determine the level of training you require. For example, if your goal is to become a CNE and you have been working as a network administrator, then you know the administration side of NetWare but have never installed or configured a NetWare file server. Instead of spending time in the system administration course, your time would be better spent attending the service and support course. This course is where you will learn how to configure and install NetWare and the shell, and to troubleshoot the network. This route will be much more productive in reaching the goals you set than taking every course or studying everything about NetWare. You might find that no courses are necessary but some light review of the NetWare manuals is all you need. (You might want to find someone with the student manuals and study them as well. This improves your chances of passing the exams.)

When you feel you have completed studying and preparing yourself for the exams, reevaluate yourself with the skills chart. Use a different color pen when ranking yourself so you can compare your skill level now with the first time you completed the chart. If you find you are still not happy about your ranking, find the areas that need improving and concentrate on those areas. Repeat this process until you feel you know the topics cold. As you continue to find your weak points take whatever steps are necessary to become trained.

Obtaining the required financing

Financing your training is an important step in the certification process. Everyone can get financial support, but finding the correct source takes time and effort. Before you begin the actual process of funding your education, take time to figure out how much financing you need. The following points summarize the things you need to take into consideration:

- Training costs
- Testing costs
- Travel expenses
- Lost work time
- Miscellaneous expenses

The first step is to add up all the costs of classes and testing. Make sure you add a little extra for failed tests in your estimate. Even though you probably won't fail an examination if you prepare properly, it's best to plan for a failure just in case. You need this money in addition to your normal paycheck and a little bit of additional money for emergencies and miscellaneous expenses. Failure to plan ahead will certainly cost you your certification.

Also take time to consider hidden costs. For example, you need to factor in additional travel expenses if the test and training centers are further away than your usual place of work. In some cases you might need to take time off from work to attend class. Some companies will not allow you to miss work to attend class; others will ask you to make up the time by working extra hours later. If your company will not pay you during this time, you need to factor in the amount you need to pay your bills. As an alternative, you could always take vacation time. Try to think about all the possible sources of trouble and the alternatives. As you can see, there is a lot to consider in the financial arena before you even begin the process of getting financing.

There are a number of ways to get the money you need for certification training. The sources you use depend on a number of factors, including who the training will benefit and what length of time you need to pay for the training costs. Of course, the most important factor is the technique you plan to use to get the aid. Do you go to your company or simply rely on your own resources? The technique you use greatly affects your chances of success. Figure 3-2 provides you with some ideas on techniques you can use to get financial aid. As you can see, there are at least three different techniques you can use.

Some people save for training before they actually begin, that way there are no costs to burden them after they graduate. Consultants or people who plan to start their own business often use this technique. Trying to pay for your education and get a business going at the same time usually doesn't work very well. However, most people take a learn-now, pay-later approach to the whole process.

Company sponsorship is the method most people use to get certification training. Convincing your company to sponsor you is relatively easy if they just installed a LAN or the network administrator recently left the company. The need for someone to manage the LAN is usually pretty obvious by the time all the hardware and software is installed. Of course, convincing them that you're the right person for the job might prove a little more difficult. This is a situation where you need to provide proof that you can do the job, and do it better than anyone else in the company. There are other forms of sponsorship as well. For example, you might get a state or federal government agency that promotes work programs to sponsor your training. Other forms of sponsorship cover everything from veterans programs to scholarships and grants.

There are always those people who can't get total financial support from one source. These are the people who usually need to work a little harder to get anything done in their company or they might be part of a small business that can't afford the total cost of training. In this case you might need to spend time putting together a package deal. One or more sources can help you get the financing you need and reap the benefits of that training. To use this technique you get part of the support from one source, and use that source as a means to get other people to join in. For example, what if you are part of a small company? The company might recognize the need to obtain the services of a trained network administrator, but might not have the financial resources to pay for the training. If you put part of your own money into the support fund (or get a scholarship or other form of financial support), the company might provide the other part.

Some people save the money they need for education, then go to school. While this method does mean a delay in getting your training, it does reduce the after-training expenses you'll encounter. This is ideal for consultants.

3-2
Getting financial aid.

A common source of money for training is company sponsorship. You convince your company that it is in their best interest to supply the money required for training. This usually involves some type of payback period.

One option that many people don't consider is combining support from a number of sources. For example, you could get your company to support half the cost; a loan to support a quarter of the cost, and savings to support the rest.

As you can see, there are a lot of sources you can tap for financial support during your training. The technique you use to gain financial support determines which sources you try to tap. For example, many military personnel can use their GI benefits to get training. (Of course, this assumes you spent time in the military.) There are also student loans and scholarships you can use. Some of these sources will not be available, simply because you don't qualify for one reason or another. Make sure you don't waste time trying to tap a financial source that you can't possibly use.

Figure 3-3 shows you some of the sources you can use to acquire the capital required for certification training and testing. These six sources represent the ones that people most commonly use. The following paragraphs describe all these options in detail. Use your imagination and detective skills to track down other sources of potential financial support. Some jobs offer more potential sources of financial support than others. Remember, only a lack of research and motivation can prevent you from finding the financial support you need.

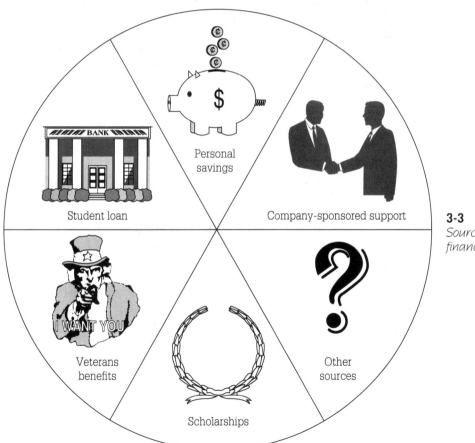

3-3
Sources of financial aid support.

Company-sponsored support

Getting financial support from a company is the most common method that people use. You usually need to provide proof that the company needs the services your training will provide and that you are the best person for the job. In most cases, you must show a willingness to repay the company by promising to work for them for a specified period of time after you complete the training. There are also instances where you will have to repay the company for moneys they expended if you fail to meet your goal. These are all considerations you need to take into account if you plan to go this route to get financial support.

At this point you might think that getting company support is an all or nothing proposition. There are a lot of different possibilities when you attempt to get support from your company. You could offer to pay for a portion of your training (or get financial assistance from another source) and ask the company to pay the rest. This shows that you are willing to invest in your own future and makes it a lot more likely that the company will help provide financial assistance. Some companies also offer interest-free education loans. Essentially you take an advance against your salary to pay for the training. Every week (or whatever your pay period is) the company takes a small portion of the loan out of your paycheck. The interest-free nature of this loan makes it especially appealing to people on a lower income scale.

Some people think that getting company support is only for full-time employees. There are many situations in which a company might consider providing educational benefits to a part-time employee as well. For example, you might qualify for the educational loan benefit described in the previous paragraph. Other scenarios include going full-time for a specific payback period or, in rare cases, showing that you will provide a very great benefit to the company with the training you get. Never limit your horizons to what you think you can get. Remember, all the company can do is say no if they don't like your proposal.

Getting a proposal together is one of the most important parts of obtaining this type of financial support. You need to prove two things. First, you need to provide proof that the company needs the services of a network administrator for their LAN. Second, you need to prove that you are the only person or the most qualified person to fill that role.

There are quite a few tools in this book that will help you get started on this proposal. The certification goals worksheet in chapter 2 (FIG. 2-1) helps you determine what you plan to achieve from this training. A goals worksheet can also show management that you are serious about obtaining the training. It can also provide you with reasons the company needs a network administrator. The skill level ranking chart in FIG. 3-1 not only shows personal weak and strong areas, but provides a basis for showing why you are the best candidate for the job. Much of the material in chapter 6 can also help you get the information needed to create a convincing proposal.

Figure 3-4 provides a sample outline you can use to get started on your proposal. Of course, you'll need to modify it to meet any company-specific requirements or to meet your own personal needs. Make sure you don't go to management empty-handed. Even if you don't write a formal proposal, you can at least get together all the answers to questions they are likely to ask. Make sure you are prepared to provide them with the best possible reasons to help you achieve your goals and provide you with the financial support you need.

Introduction
    A description of the proposal
    A synopsis of any relevant company rules, regulations, or benefits
    Definitions of terms and acronyms
How will this training benefit the company?
    Demonstrated need for a network administrator
    Cost/benefits analysis
    Resident LAN expert available at all times
What am I willing to provide the company in exchange for the training?
Why am I the best person for the job?
    Existing skills
    Existing training
    Training goals
    Personality traits
    Other considerations
Conclusion

3-4
Sample company financial aid proposal outline.

As you can see, there are a number of things that you need to put in the proposal. The introduction allows you to quickly summarize the reasons you put the proposal together. Make sure you include any relevant company rules or guidelines. You also need to define any nonstandard terms you use within this section. Likewise, the conclusion summarizes the contents of the proposal. It doesn't contain a repeat of the information the proposal contains; it simply summarizes the high points of your proposal. A manager should get a good idea of what you are trying to say by reading the introduction and conclusion of the proposal. Then, if they want more details, they can read the contents of the proposal.

There are three main sections in the body of this outline; your outline might include more. The first thing you need to do is concentrate on the needs of the company. Show management that you are thinking of the company first, yourself second. The first part of the section tells them about their need to have a network administrator available. Of course, one of the first questions that comes to mind is why not use an outside consultant to perform this work. You need to demonstrate the need to keep a staff administrator. One way to do this appears in the second part of this section. Showing management that it is actually cheaper to maintain a staff network administrator is one way to prove your point. There are also intangible benefits you can cite. For example, one intangible benefit is the security of knowing that no one outside the company has access to vital data. This information appears in the third part of this section.

The second section of the proposal tells management what you are willing to exchange for the financial support. Of course, what you offer is up to you. The standard items include a promise to stay with the company for a specific length of time or other concessions. Make sure you let management know that you are willing to negotiate. If you offer something they don't want, and you make it obvious you are not willing to negotiate, then your proposal will fail even if management is interested in getting a trained network administrator on staff. Don't kill your chances of becoming certified by being inflexible or unimaginative.

The third section of the proposal must concentrate on you. Tell management why you are the best person for the job. This is the place where you can brag about your capabilities a little bit (don't brag too much though). Initially, concentrate on tangible evidence such as your current job skills and training. Then let management know about your training goals. Showing them the tangible parts of your plan makes it obvious that you want to succeed in your certification goals. Finally, you can tell them about the intangible benefits you can offer the company. For example, are you good at working with people? Make sure you offer management some evidence of this intangible skill. Does your work record demonstrate that you're a hard worker? Make sure you let management know about this too.

As you can see, writing a financial support proposal requires an investment of time and effort. The results are well worth the effort though. Getting your certification can open new doors of opportunity that you might not get otherwise. In addition, some of the work you need to do for the proposal is a direct result of the work you need to do for certification anyway. Many of the pieces of information you need to convince management to provide you with financial support already appear in other areas of this book. You can also use them for other certification goals.

There are many sources you can tap for student loans, even though most people look no further than their local bank. Of course, the number and type of sources vary by region of the country and your personal situation. So the first objective is to find out where you can get a student loan. The following paragraphs provide some pointers you can use in this area.

- In most cases your local college or university can supply you with this information. Just look in the student catalogs or other brochures provided by them. The writers of these books pack them with great ideas for finding financial aid. (Obviously the college or university wants to make it as easy as possible for someone to attend; you're simply using this source of information for another purpose.)
- You should also check with friends. You might be surprised at the bits of information you find out this way.
- Life insurance companies and other financial planning institutions also make good places to check for this type of information.

Once you determine where you can get a student loan, you need to find out the criteria for getting the loan. For example, any student loan will require that you provide evidence of income. A government loan might require that you fall below a specific income level, while a bank loan might require that you exceed a specific income level. The one loan that might require the least financial information is a student loan provided by an insurance company or fraternal organization. In most cases you secure this type of loan with your insurance policy or other tangible assets.

You need to take other things into consideration with a student loan as well. For example, what type of payback period does the institution offer and how high is the interest. By shopping around you can usually optimize these features to your benefit. Especially important is the interest rate. Even waiting a few days can change the amount of interest you pay on a loan. A check on the stability of the bank or other lending institution is important too, because most loans contain a clause that forces you to pay back the entire loan in one lump sum should the lending institution request it. Consider any stipulations that the lender might have about the loan. For example, some lenders might require that you provide proof of schooling in the form of a graduation certificate. You need to find out everything you can about the institution, what types of loans they offer, and what you can expect from them in the way of payment plans.

Of course, you also need to consider what you can afford. Unfortunately, some people find that they get into more debt than they can repay (as witnessed by the number of government student loans that remain unpaid). Make sure you aren't taking out too large a loan for your

Student loans

education. If you don't plan ahead, you might find yourself living on peanut butter and jelly sandwiches for a long time before you get the loan repaid. Even worse, you might end up filing for bankruptcy. A little planning goes a long way toward ensuring that you achieve your goals without worrying about money all the time.

Now comes the important part of the process. Once you decide on a particular lender, get all the paperwork filled out. They usually require a lot of financial information. For example, a potential lender will want to know where you work and live in addition to what you make. The best idea is to get a copy of the loan application and fill it out at home if possible. That way you will have all the required information at your fingertips. After you get the form filled out, take it back to the lender. Take any required documentation with you as well. For example, some lenders require that you bring in a pay stub or other proof of income. They might require that you bring in a birth certificate and other forms of identification as well. Make sure you ask the lender about these requirements when you get the loan forms.

Scholarships   The number and variety of scholarships available to you are probably limited when compared with other forms of education. Unlike your local college or university, it is doubtful that your local NAEC will have any type of scholarship plan available. Most scholarships are tied to a specific institution of learning. A scholarship gets created when someone endows a university or college with the money required to fund it.

Don't let the paucity of scholarships deter you from exploring this avenue of financial aid. Fortunately there are a few other places to get scholarships that could help in this situation. For example, many life insurance companies and fraternal organizations provide scholarships. Some of these scholarships are aimed at technical schooling rather than more traditional subjects. Your local church or other organizations might have scholarships available as well. In many cases there are very few stipulations placed on these scholarships by the people setting up the fund. A check with the leaders of these organizations might reveal a scholarship that very few people know about.

Unfortunately, most of these scholarships are fairly small. Most of them will pay for one or perhaps two of the courses you require for certification. If you go this route, plan on supplementing your scholarship funds with money from personal savings or other sources. In many cases a scholarship offers just the right amount of additional funding to get company support for your educational needs. This is especially true of smaller companies that want the services of a network administrator but lack the funds for training. As you can see, even if the scholarship is small, it can make the difference between getting and not getting your education.

Once you get a scholarship, make sure you understand all the qualifications. For example, many scholarships require that you pass the course before you receive payment from the scholarship fund. You need to supply proof that you passed the course in the form of a graduation or other type of certificate. If this is true, you will have to pay for your certification course from a savings account, then reimburse the account when you receive the scholarship money. (Most NAECs require that you pay for your classes in advance.) Some scholarships have other types of requirements or restrictions on their use to specific types of education. Make sure you understand all these requirements before you use the money you expect to receive from a scholarship. In some cases, failure to observe a specific requirement could result in the loss of scholarship moneys.

Veterans' benefits

It's amazing how few veterans actually use their GI benefits to further their education, especially when you consider the time they spent in the service to get these benefits. The perception is that veterans' educational benefits are only for college, not for technical or vocational training. However, there are many forms of technical/vocational training that qualify for these educational benefits as well.

There are a few things that you will need to prepare for if you use veterans' benefits. First, there is the usual amount of ever-changing government paperwork to fill out. Make sure you talk to your local VA representative well in advance to get all the required paperwork. Spend some time learning how to fill it out correctly. Also make sure the certification training qualifies for VA benefits, because the requirements for these programs change on an almost continual basis.

Once you determine that you qualify, the training qualifies, and that you have all the paperwork filled out correctly, make sure your local NAEC will accept government payment. Some NAECs require payment in advance of the course. You will need to work out some type of arrangement with the NAEC because the government pays only after you successfully complete the course. Unfortunately, they also pay the educational institution directly. You might need to spend some time working with the NAEC on this issue.

Personal savings

All the previous methods of getting financial aid had one thing in common; someone else paid the bills for your training. Of course, this is the best way to pay for your training, but it doesn't always work out that way. If you do plan to pay for all or part of your training using your own financial resources, make sure you have enough to complete your training before you even start. This is a good rule because it is all too common for someone to start certification training, only to drop out later due to a lack of funds. In fact, the best plan is to make sure you have all your bills covered, plus a little for emergencies, plus the total amount required for certification class and testing. Remember, paying for the classes isn't the end of your financial responsibility. You also need to set aside the money required for testing and continuing education.

There are other sources of personal income that you can tap besides your savings account. For example, some people have paid-up life insurance policies that they can borrow against. In many cases, the money contained in these policies can pay for the entire schooling process. The interest on such a loan is usually fairly low, almost always below the rate you'll get from a bank or other financial institution. In essence, an insurance loan is one where you borrow from yourself.

You can also take money out of an IRA or other long-term savings account if you're willing to pay the penalties and don't want to wait until you have the money saved in your regular savings account. Of course, you need to spend some time with your bank working out the details of this solution. The penalties and other legal considerations vary by bank and savings plan.

One final solution to get the last bit of support you need is to pay for part of your classes using a credit card. Many people pay for their classes using a credit card, then pay off the credit card company through their monthly bill. Of course, to pay the entire cost of certification classes and testing using a credit card, you need a fairly high line of credit. The big disadvantage to this method is the high interest rate you'll pay for your training. On the other hand, you might need to get the training today rather than tomorrow to take advantage of an opportunity.

Other programs   There are other payment programs you can use. For example, some states and the federal government have job training plans for minorities (in addition to student loans and other forms of assistance you must repay). If you qualify for one of these plans, then the money you receive can pay for all or part of your schooling costs. As with the veterans' benefits mentioned earlier, there is usually a lot of paperwork involved with this approach. Make sure you know all the requirements before you sign up for any classes. In most cases you'll need to combine the money you get from these programs with some other type of financial aid package. For example, your company might help pay for part of the cost if you can get government support for the other part. In fact, the personnel office of your company is a good place to begin your search for appropriate aid programs.

You might be able to get grants from corporations or other organizations in exchange for some type of consideration. For example, a consultant might get a grant from a company in exchange for free maintenance service for a specific length of time. Of course, it takes time and effort to ferret out these sources of financial aid. You might want to consider this as a final option if all the other plans in this section fail to produce results.

Who do you talk to about training?

You realize the need for training of some sort. So where and who do you talk to about obtaining the proper training? The proper training is essential to obtaining the level of expertise needed to complete your goal of certification. The level of certification you wish to acquire, along with the level of experience and knowledge you currently have, will help you decide on the type of training needed. Thus far we have helped you understand what your skill and knowledge levels are; we will now look at where and how to obtain training.

Training comes in many different ways and from many different sources. The type of training that will best suit your needs depends on your personal work and study habits. In many cases the best idea is to obtain your training from job experience. This is referred to as on-the-job training. In other cases the best means of training is to attend a structured course. Other types of training include third-party lectures, videotapes, audiotapes, self-study manuals, instructor-led classes, and of course the trial-and-error method.

Hands-on training

At times the on-the-job training method of education might be the best way of obtaining information. It can also be the most time-consuming method. While this type of training will supply you with the most hands-on, real-world way of performing a task, the amount of time you must invest before you have enough information to become certified might take years. This is not to say that if you do not have on-the-job training you cannot pass the certification, or if you are working for an organization that you will not become certified for a long time. It simply means that no matter how much knowledge you obtain from other sources, nothing will replace the knowledge acquired from on-the-job experience.

The best place to acquire on-the-job training is, of course, to find a job that's related to your education requirements. This might not be a very easy task. Usually, before you can get hired by a company, you must have the same skills that you are trying to learn. If this is the case, you might have to work out an arrangement with the prospective employer to work as an entry-level employee or to work at a reduced rate. You might be able to work out an arrangement to assist on projects free of charge in return for the hands-on experience. While this is not putting any money into your pocket, you will be getting the necessary training you are looking for. Consider it as a payment towards your education.

When you start to look for places of employment, either on a training basis or as a permanent placement, remember that you are not locked into a long-term permanent job. If at some point in time you find that you are not learning what you need to learn or that you are not happy where you are, you can always find another job that will give you what you are looking for. Just because you are trying to get an education or are currently certified, you do not have to stay at a place you are not happy with. If you are not happy or comfortable with your situation, you will not be as apt to learn what you need to know as quickly as if you really enjoyed the job.

So where and how do you start to look for this job? The place to start should be to check your personal resources. These are people that might be in a position to help you. They can include family members, friends, neighbors, or people you work with. Often these people will not be able to directly help you, but they might know of someone that knows someone that will be able to help you. You will then have a lead, and a name that you can use as a possible reference and as an icebreaker. The more people you let know what you are doing and what you are looking for, the better your chances are of getting that warm lead. The more personal contact you have with a prospective employer, the higher your chances are of obtaining a position.

Another place to turn to for a prospective employer for on-the-job training is the help wanted section of the newspaper. This source of leads will point you to employers that have a need for some type of assistance. You will find that this is usually a tougher way to land a position than finding a warm, and personal, lead. There will probably be many people that apply for the same position and often some of the applicants are better qualified or overqualified for the position. This will make it very difficult for you to get very far. You might need to find some type of angle to make your services more attractive. This can include working at a lower pay rate or signing on with the company for a long time.

Other sources to look at for on-the-job training would be job services, job counselors, employment agencies, and head-hunter services. These are all good places to contact for opportunities. You will more than likely find that they will want or need someone with some type of experience. You are again caught in the loop of not being able to find a job without experience, and not being able to get experience without a job. The final way to find the on-the-job training you need is to knock on doors. Look in the phone book for computer and Novell dealers in your area and then visit them. The in-person approach normally yields the best results. You are presenting yourself to the possible employer so that they can see what you are like. They can talk face to face with you and get to know you. You will also be able to present your situation to them in a way you can't over the phone. Remember, you must create a reason why they should hire or help you. You must create an incentive for the company to hire you.

The best way to get the training needed and bring yourself up to speed is to enroll in a professional education program. The courses will present you with much information in a class that only lasts a couple of days. The instructor will normally present you with a series of lectures along with oral or written question-and-answer periods, lab exercises, and hands-on experience.

Instructor-led training

Instructor-led courses are available from a variety of different sources. These sources include Novell, NAECs, colleges, universities, vendors, and different third-party educational facilities. Each of these different educational facilities provides a vast myriad of services. The services offered by these facilities range from the very general to very specific. The lengths of the programs also range from just a few hours to four or more years. The costs of the different educational services ranges from nothing to thousands of dollars.

Because the educational facilities vary in class size, materials offered, length of program, cost, and types of services, you will need to consult with them for your needs. To locate the different institutes in your area, check the phone book, talk to your local chamber of commerce, and check with local computer dealers. Often local computer dealers will be able to tell you where the best place in town is to get training. Because they are in the trade and see many of the qualified people working in the industry, they will know which institute has the best reputation.

The best place to obtain the required information for Novell certifications is from an NEAC. Novell makes excellent training available for their certifications, as well as their line of products. While Novell does offer some training directly, most of the training comes from NAECs. Novell authorizes the centers to teach their courses at a strict level of quality. Novell inspects the centers for proper hardware and software, as well as the general overall condition of the facility. Each center must use Certified NetWare Instructors (CNIs) to teach the courses. These instructors have passed a series of competency exams and have attended special courses designed to make sure that they meet the Novell standards for teaching the course.

NAECs are located worldwide, with the largest concentration being in the United States. Some of the NAECs are quite large with upwards of 10 classrooms in one location. There are also a few NAEC companies that have education centers in different parts of the country. The centers are all basically the same because Novell must authorize each one and each center must meet the Novell guidelines. What distinguishes the different centers from each other is the quality of the instructors. While each instructor is Novell certified, many of the instructors teach only what is in the Novell course manuals. While this is the base information required for Novell certifications, it might not always lend itself to real-world experiences. The "extras" that the better instructors include usually come from years in the field practicing what they teach. We have all had an instructor or professor that really knew the book material they were teaching, but ask them a question that is not part of the manual and they haven't got a clue. When selecting the education center you want to attend, be sure to ask for references from past students. Talk to these people and get a feel for how the instructor handled the class, subject matter, and questions about related topics not included in the course material. You will find that most of the instructors will get good reviews.

Another item that separates the NAECs is the courses they offer. Many of the classes require the latest in computer technology, and some of the smaller NAECs cannot justify the expense of the equipment. These centers are then left teaching only the basic core classes. This is okay for the basic certifications, but if you want to become a CNE or ECNE then you will have to find an NAEC that offers the advanced classes. The number and frequency of courses is also an issue. If the class that you want to attend is offered only quarterly you might have to wait a few months before attending the class. Some of the larger NAECs offer most of the core classes on a monthly rotation and the advanced classes on a four- to six-week rotation.

Whether you attend a large or small NAEC, you will be receiving quality training by some of the most credible institutes around. Novell has long been recognized by the industry for their proactive approach to training their dealers, users, and technicians. You can always count on the course materials written for their software to be current with what's on the market. (With the advancements in the industry made almost daily, the course materials are maintained as current as possible.) To get a list of the Novell Authorized Education Centers in your area, you can call Novell directly at 1-800-NETWARE (1-800-638-9273) or the Novell FaxBack service at 1-800-233-3382 or 1-801-429-5363. Both of these numbers will get you in touch with either the Novell education group or the FaxBack service. You will then have the opportunity to order a list of NAECs. The list will be sent to your fax machine free of charge.

Novell, as well as other sources, offers self-study programs. The self-study programs are good for the self-starting person that has both the time and attitude to study on their own. By using the self-study programs offered by Novell and the NAECs you can save yourself a few dollars. The courses are designed to supply you with the course manuals offered by Novell and usually include some form of lab training. Most of the NAECs will send you all the course manuals so that you can study them at a time that is convenient for you. After you have had some time to study the manuals, usually a month or so, you will then attend some type of lab session. This lab session is usually one week and has a CNI present. The instructor might lead you in different exercises or lectures depending on how the NAEC structures the class. If you have any questions or problems during the exercises, the instructor is there to help you in any way possible.

Self-study training

The self-study programs are an excellent way to get the training, hands-on experience, and knowledge needed to obtain Novell certification. They will save you money by not having to attend the more expensive instructor-led courses. If you decide to participate in the self-study program, to make it work for you, be sure you are 100 percent dedicated to reaching your goal. The biggest disadvantage to the self-study program is the amount of individual work it takes to prepare yourself. You will not have the luxury of a structured class and an instructor that will lead you by the hand through each chapter of the manuals. You will have to devote at least two hours a day to studying the Novell manuals and researching any questions you have about the subject matter. Before you attend the lab session of the program, you need to know the book material completely. The lab session will provide you with the resources to bring together all the loose ends and answer any questions you might have about the operating system, installation, software, hardware, concepts, or any other area dealing with networks.

To find out more about the self-study certification programs, contact your local NAEC, your local computer dealer, or call Novell. The programs will vary from education center to education center, so be sure to thoroughly investigate what each has to offer.

Often the standard approach to training, such as on-the-job training and attending classes, does not always fit into our schedules. For this reason alternative forms of education are very popular. Alternative forms of

Other types of training

education might include books, audiotapes, videotapes, and computer-based training (CBT) programs. These are all excellent sources of information that will help to augment the training process.

From the experienced computer technician down to the beginner, a bookcase with a wide variety of computer books is a necessity. This library will prove to be a great asset in your quest for advancement in the computer industry. With a well-rounded library you will be able to reference the topics and subjects you might not know very well. You will find that your library will grow immensely in a short time. Many of the books you get will have just a few pages on the subject that concerns you right now, but will provide a source of reference on other material in the future.

There are many books written about the Novell NetWare operating system on the bookshelves of your local bookstores. Many of these books are very general in nature, with the same material included in books supplied by Novell. They are usually someone's interpretation of the subject. In some cases they are more concise than the books Novell has written. Most of these books go into great detail on how to install the operating system and how to manage the system once NetWare's been installed. If you attended the Novell courses you will find this to be a repeat of the information the instructor presented in class. On the other hand, these Novell-specific books are very helpful in teaching you about the system if you have not had any formal training or on-the-job experience with NetWare. If you are new to the world of NetWare, you will find that these books will help supplement your knowledge.

There is another good reason to buy some of these general Novell books for your library. The Novell classes focus on the current operating systems. This is great for learning about the latest systems that are being sold, but you will find that many businesses still have old versions of the operating systems. These old versions serve the businesses with everything they need. There is no reason for them to spend money on a new system. In their mind a new version of the operating system will not provide them with anything they don't already have. As a Novell expert you will need to know about the early versions of NetWare and how they work. You should know the different commands and the different terminology that was a part of the old versions of NetWare. There are many differences in the versions of NetWare. Version 2.0a is different from NetWare 2.2 and NetWare 4.0. This is one reason why books written about the different operating systems will be an asset to your library. It is sometimes difficult, if not impossible, to get books from Novell on past operating systems.

Don't ignore the general networking books. Many of these books have a lot of practical information about how to administer your network. (See *Hands-On Guide to Network Management* by John Mueller and Robert Williams (Windcrest # 4418) for more information about network administration in general.) While these books might not provide Novell-specific information, they will help you gain a better understanding of networks in general. Even if you don't use this information immediately, you will find it essential later.

To find books on the Novell operating system (or networks in general) you do not need to go very far. Most bookstores carry at least a few. The large bookstore chains normally carry a good line of Novell books written by many different authors. Many computer stores carry one or two different ones as well. You will find that in most large cities there will be a technical bookstore that specializes in computer books. Most of these stores will carry most of the books written about the NetWare operating system. You can normally find a list of the bookstores in your area by looking in the yellow pages of your phone book. Another good source about where to find computer books is to talk to the Novell instructors in your area. They normally stay current with information on different computer related topics. They also visit the more technical bookstores on an ongoing basis to help stay current with technology. You will also find that most of the more technical bookstores will supply you with a list of titles that they have access to, and will ship books anywhere in the world to you.

Besides books, another great source of training material is the use of audio- and videotapes. Both Novell and third-party companies make tapes that are basically the Novell courses. These tapes will supply you with a great deal of information about NetWare, but are usually fairly expensive. While the cost makes them out of reach for most individuals, they are good for companies that need to train a few people in their organization. They can buy one tape and let all of their employees use it. This is a lot more cost effective than sending all of their employees to a certification class. A note here for companies that might plan to do this; send one person to the certification course or have a person that knows NetWare. You will find that the tapes present a lot of material, but they will not be able to answer the questions that arise from watching the tape.

Novell offers a vast array of tapes on different NetWare topics. The tapes include both basic and advanced topics. Novell has had the tapes professionally done and continues to update them as new products are released. You can order the tapes from Novell or from your Novell dealer. To get a list of tapes offered by Novell, call the Novell FaxBack service or your Novell dealer.

Novell also offers a computer-based training program that will help you train for your certifications, as well as just give you a better understanding of NetWare. These programs provide information that you read and then exercises that require input from the reader (sort of a mini-exam that you can use to test your knowledge). These are good programs that will help you understand the workings of NetWare. However, they usually stimulate many other questions not addressed by the program. The programs are also quite expensive, but are very attractive for companies that need to train more than one person. To get a list of available computer-based training programs and their part numbers, call the Novell FaxBack service or contact your Novell authorized dealer.

Getting the most from your training

As you have seen, there are many different approaches to training for becoming a certified Novell expert and for general knowledge of the computer industry. It is normal to feel a bit overwhelmed because of the vast amount of information you will receive in preparation for your certification exams. The best advice available to help you obtain your certification is to stay focused. By using the goals worksheet presented in chapter 2 and the information presented here in chapter 3, you will be able to formulate what your goals are and how to obtain them. Keep your goals worksheet with you all the time and look at it often. This will keep you focused.

To get the most from your training you will also want to take the training one step at a time. It becomes very easy to get caught up in the frenzy of trying to learn as much as you can as fast as you can. Take one topic at a time and work with it until you feel you know the subject matter. Don't try to learn all the other related subtopics that are part of the main topic. You will find that every topic or subject has many other related subtopics and each one of them has many other related topics and subtopics as well. Soon you will find that the subject you had originally started to study is replaced by a new topic and you have not learned anything more about the original item of study. Take one item at a time and stick with it until finished.

Another good way to get the most from your training is to take notes. If you are in a class you will want to take brief notes. Do not take notes on everything the instructor says. If you do this you will find that you miss a lot. You might not even catch enough of the discussion to ask questions. Try to write just the keywords that are being used, then after the class is over or at a break period you can fill in some of the other information. Usually just the keywords will start a thought process that will replay the lecture in your mind. At this point you can write down as much information as you like. You will have the time and be able to concentrate on how to convert the information from a thought to a written idea.

When reading the books and manuals use a highlighter and sticky notes for references. Many people highlight sections of the text that they know; what you should be highlighting are the parts that you don't know or the parts you need additional help on. Once you highlight the text use the sticky notes to mark the page for future reference.

You will find that one of the best ways to study the course manuals is to break the process down into three parts. First, quickly read the material in a summary fashion. Don't spend much time reading the material; you only want to get familiar with the content of the book. For example, you might want to scan the headings and the first sentence of each paragraph. This will help you understand the author's intent in writing the book. Second, get a note pad, your sticky notes, and your highlighter. Then reread the manuals, making notes and highlighting the important information as well as the information that is new to you or that you do not understand. The third step is to study your notes and the marked pages and then research any areas you do not understand.

Using this process takes a little more time than other techniques, but you will find that you will retain a lot more information. There is something special about converting information from a thought in your mind to letters on a piece of paper. The final step in this process will be different for each of you. You might want to reread the manual and your notes again. If you feel you know the material, consider taking the exams. You have to make that decision when you get to that point and it might change with each manual you read.

The secret to making this work and passing the exams is to find the style, type of training, and studying technique that best stimulates your mind. This might take some time and you might have to change your approach several times. Be aware of what techniques work for you and which techniques produce the best results.

When doing your studying you will find that a short burst of studying will produce better results than long periods of intense concentration. Remember the long all-night "cram" sessions preparing for high school and college exams? All this did was put your mind in a state of exhaustion. More likely than not, you didn't retain any of the information you studied. You will be able to concentrate longer and remember better if have a rested mind. You will find too that your exam scores will be higher if you take the test when you are rested and alert.

When doing your studying, hit it hard for ten to fifteen minutes then take a short break. Your actual study time will vary from day to day. It also varies from person to person. The best rule of thumb is to study until your mind starts to wander. The moment your mind starts to wander you aren't getting any real work done; it's time to take a break. Get up and walk around, get a drink of water or a breath of fresh air. You will find that your concentration will be much higher and your retention will also be better. If you study for hours on end, your concentration is usually high at the start and near the end. Most of the information in between becomes diluted. Short-burst studying prevents your mind from getting overwhelmed and tired.

Other study techniques include the use of flash cards, posters, and recording your notes on a cassette tape. All these methods are proven ways to study and improve your knowledge base. When using flash cards, use 3-by-5 cards with a question on one side and a complete answer on the other. You can use these while stuck in traffic, watching TV, or just about any time. You can also give them to a friend and have them ask you questions. Posters are similar to flash cards. Get a package of poster paper and a large dark marker. On the poster write just a few keywords, then hang the poster in your home or office. The keywords that you put on the poster should start a thought process that gets you thinking about some subject. Flash cards and posters will not only help you in studying for the exams by using them over and over, but the process of making them also reinforces the concepts in your mind.

The use of cassette tapes is another way to get the most from your training. By recording your notes on a cassette, you can play the tapes over and over at any time. They are especially useful while you are driving; just play them in your car's tape player. You will find that by listening to your notes in your own voice, your mind will retain more. You can also reuse the tapes for different classes and different manuals. You can also use the tape recorder to record lectures while in class. You can then replay the course lectures at your convenience and at your own pace. Often you will find that you missed something the instructor said. This is especially true if the material is new to you. As you are thinking about what is being presented, the instructor moves on to another subject and you miss some part of what is being said.

All the mentioned training techniques will help you to reach your goal of certification, if you apply them. By staying focused on your goals, selecting a training program that's acceptable, and applying the proper study techniques and refining them to your style, you will find yourself prepared for the exams.

Conclusion

As you can see, learning the trade is much more involved than just reading some books, attending a couple of classes, and getting a little on-the-job experience. To be truly successful you must move beyond the average person who calls themselves an expert or a CNE. We know that these "experts" are nothing more than box movers or basic installers. What separates you from the others will be the extra education that you pursue.

This education may come from upgrading your CNA certification to a CNE, ECNE, or CNI from Novell. It can come from obtaining a degree from a college or university in your area. Other ways to obtain the needed education are on-the-job training, the trial-and-error method, or attending night classes, seminars, or vendor training.

The type of training that best satisfies your needs and goals will be dictated by what your job requirements are and what you expect to accomplish in your career. Remember that to stay competitive with the average person in this industry you must do your homework. This includes reading the trade papers and working with the products. To be a real expert and the person that all the companies want, you must take the initiative to further your education and experience. Whatever type of education is right for you, make the investment and follow it through, it will be well worth it.

4 Taking the tests

Taking tests is the least favorite part of any training experience; they seem to evoke the worst feelings from all of us. While general exams are difficult, professional examinations are more difficult than just about any other examination you can take. With most general exams you have a wide range of study aids available. If nothing else, you have a group of fellow students to talk with. Professional exams usually don't offer these aids; usually only a small group of people interested in something more than just a general knowledge of the world around them takes these types of exams. Novell's examinations are no different. Not only are there a lack of third-party study aids, but each exam is totally different. Therefore, you can't even rely on the input from fellow students to help very much.

The emotional pressures of a professional exam are a lot greater than a general exam as well. Of course, the reason emotions run the gamut from agony to ecstasy is easy to understand. The stakes are high—a career is up for grabs. Every professional exam you take has the potential of helping your career if you pass it, or reducing your potential if you don't.

Learning to take an exam is just like any other skill; you gain the knowledge to perform the task, practice until you become proficient, then demonstrate your ability. To become a proficient test taker you learn how to study, how to think when taking the exam, and how to prepare yourself emotionally. This chapter takes a look at all these elements and more. It helps you prepare for the Novell exams not only at the knowledge level, but at the emotional level as well.

There is another event you have to prepare for as well. Even if you go through all the training courses, study hard, and take the proper approach to testing, there is a good chance you will fail at least one examination. After all, if there wasn't a chance of failure, what would be the value of getting certified? The potential for failure helps differentiate between those who really want the professional recognition that comes with certification and those who don't. Dealing with that failure is an important element of passing the exam the next time. Looking for places you made mistakes in the first attempt will help you prepare for the second attempt.

This chapter helps you prepare for the three areas of testing by telling you how to study and what to study. It also stresses the importance of taking the Novell viewpoint when answering questions. Most important of all, this chapter helps you over the ultimate hurdle, dealing with failure. The better prepared you are to take the test, the more devastating the failure becomes. Helping you get back on your feet again is a very important feature of this chapter.

Gathering the information you'll need

The student guides you receive while taking the Novell courses listed in TABLE 1-1 are your most important asset in taking an exam; especially if you take good notes during class. There are two operative phrases here. First, you must take the Novell courses to obtain the Novell view of networking. Second, you must take good notes in class. Unless you perform both of these steps, there is a good chance that you will fail at least once for each exam. The reason for this failure is simple. While you might have a great understanding of networks in general, you need to know the Novell way of doing things to pass the exam.

The importance of the Novell courses

Your instructor is specially trained to help you understand networking from a Novell perspective. A Novell certification is a credential that tells the world you know what you're talking about when it comes to Novell networks. This implies that you know the Novell way of doing things. While you could argue that there are probably many other ways of performing a specific task, the certification implies that Novell has provided you with training in the Novell way of doing it.

It might seem that prescribing one way of doing things when there are many other equally correct ways of doing them is unnecessarily restrictive and oppressive. However, Novell cannot test everyone's method of doing a task, yet they must ensure that the methods used by the people they certify are correct. Another course would make people ask, "Why should I trust anyone you certify to maintain my network?" As you can see, what might seem restrictive at first, is simply a way of ensuring that everyone can perform networking tasks in a way that works every time. It also ensures that someone certified by Novell uses techniques that have been fully tested in a real-world environment. When people hire you based on your certification, what they are really hiring is someone who knows the Novell way of performing a task, an extension of Novell if you will.

So how does this relate to test taking? Because Novell must test your ability to maintain a network, and we have seen there is a logical reason for everyone performing those tasks in the same way, it follows that Novell will test that one way of doing things. If you walk into the examination room without a knowledge of Novell's way of performing a task, then there is no way for you to answer the questions correctly. (The passing requirements are high enough to void just about any possibility of someone guessing their way through the exam.) This is the first point you must remember. When you take a Novell certification exam, you are getting tested on your knowledge of Novell's way of performing a task, not your networking knowledge in general. This is a very important concept to grasp. Failure to grasp it could cost you the exam.

By now you're saying, "But Jane over there never went through the courses and she passed the exams without any problem." There is a simple reason for that as well. Some tasks can be performed only one way. When you come across questions that ask about that one way, you will find that you can answer them even if you haven't gone through the Novell courses. This is how some people get by without taking the Novell courses. They learn enough about the Novell methods to pass the exam based on their own knowledge. Of course, these are the same people who usually have several years of networking experience and a few degrees as well. Unfortunately, unless you are very skilled in networking, approaching the exams this way can prove costly. Failure to prepare yourself costs you both time and money paid for failed exams.

The other information you need before you can study for an exam is a set of good notes. What is the difference between good notes and bad ones? Actually there are no bad notes (with the exception of wrong information). There are good notes that help you study, and ones that won't. While both convey information, one doesn't provide the correct type of input.

Taking good notes

Notes are somewhat difficult to quantify until you actually need to use them. You might think something the instructor said is of the greatest importance during class, only to find that you never use the information afterward. Watching what information you use and what information you don't is one way to improve your note-taking skills. Everyone differs in their ability to retain information. One person might need to write just about everything they hear down on paper or they will not remember later, while another person might fail to hear an important fact because they are too busy taking notes.

Part of the problem is levels of concentration. How well do you concentrate? Can you work on complex problems for hours without getting mentally tired? Do you remember what you read in trade journals long after the information is no longer useful? You might find that taking a minimum of notes and really concentrating on what the instructor has to say is your best method of retaining information. In fact, some people don't take any notes at all during class. They save that activity for after class as a technique for going back over the information the instructor presented.

If you find that you can't remember anything without writing it down, you might want to consider two other methods of taking notes. Some people use the outline approach. They write quick notes about what the instructor said as an outline on a separate sheet of paper. This allows the note taker to concentrate on what the instructor has to say. After class these people fill in the outline. This helps reinforce what the instructor said during class.

Another group can actually concentrate on two things at once. They can write complete notes and still pay attention to what the instructor is saying. This is the same group of people you find talking on the telephone while working away on their computer. This is a talent that some people possess, and you can use it to good effect in class. Make sure you use every resource to ensure you get a good set of notes to study from later.

A final group of people need to resort to high technology to make sure they get all the facts. Simply take a tape recorder with you to class, record what the instructor has to say, and transcribe it later. This tends to reinforce the lessons you learn in class and still allows you to get complete notes. (Make sure you ask the instructor's permission before you start recording the session; some instructors object to the use of recording equipment in class.)

As you can see, there are a variety of ways to take notes. This is the first thing you must learn to do. Get the information down on paper so you can use it later to study. If you find that you cannot remember what the instructor said at the end of the day, you might be using the wrong note-taking technique. You should rely on your notes as an aid to memory, not as a replacement for your memory. Force your brain to do a little of the work required to remember what the instructor said during the day. Work with a variety of methods until you find the one that works best for you.

The second part of this note-taking procedure is to take notes that you will actually use. This differentiates a good note from one that you took and don't need. Taking good notes always helps you in the long run; the other kind of note is a waste of time. Unfortunately, this is something that you learn from experience. A valuable note for one person might not provide any information for someone else. Here are some rules you can follow to maximize the possibility that the notes you take are as useful as possible.

- Take complete notes. Never write down just a few words without filling the note out later. This is especially important if you use the outline approach to note taking. Some people take good notes during class, but fail to fill them out immediately afterward. When they try to use the notes to study for an exam or as part of their work later, they find the notes are incomplete or indecipherable.
- Take specific notes. Don't talk about generalities in your notes. Always make them as specific as possible. If the instructor provides an example in class, adding this example to your notes can help you get the most out of the notes later. Making the notes specific also helps trigger the memory process later. We tend to remember specific, not general, occurrences.
- Don't take notes out of context. Always provide enough surrounding information so you can get the full flavor of the note. Never jot down a quick idea that you could misinterpret later. Always provide yourself with all the details. Have you ever heard of the guy who took notes about preparing a chicken for dinner? One of the notes said, "Cut off head." So he cut off his own head instead of the chicken's head. Don't let this happen to you; take complete notes that give you the whole story.

As you can see, note taking is an important part of the learning process. Always increase your chances of passing an exam by taking good notes in class. Take the time to check the usefulness of your notes after you write them. If you find that you don't use the contents of a note later, then don't waste the time required to take that type of note again. In addition, if you find that you can almost but not quite remember something the instructor said, it is a sure sign that you needed to take a note. Make sure you remember to record this type of information during courses you take in the future.

The test taker's study guide

You're sitting at a table or desk, your student manuals on one side and a stack of notes on the other. What do you do now? What is the best way to study for your certification exam? This question plagues just about anyone who takes an exam. If you leave your study area and go to the exam with this feeling, you might actually psyche yourself into failing it. To pass the exam you must feel certain of your facts. Of course, studying too much is equally fatal. Banging your brain against the wall is not a good idea just before taking an exam. So the question remains, how much studying is too much or not enough? The following paragraphs help you find a level of study that meets your needs, yet doesn't provide too much study time. Finding the level and proper way to study is the ultimate goal to ensure you pass your exam.

Determining your best study time and length

Some people try to cram everything in the student manuals into just one or two days of study. While this might work for a short course, it probably won't do much good for a longer exam. There are two things you need to do to ensure you get the maximum benefit from your study time: control the starting time and control the length of study time. Controlling the starting time is important because that influences how you approach your study time. Controlling the length of study time ensures that you maximize the effect of your study time. The following rules should help you in both regards.

- Always study when you feel well rested; never study when you feel tired. Not only are you apt to get facts that you study confused when you feel tired, but you will remember them for a shorter length of time. Studying with a clear mind helps you remember the facts you learn for a longer period of time. Studying when you feel well rested also improves your attitude.
- Try to study at the same time each day. This helps you develop a study habit rather than forcing you to go through the inconvenience of studying. It also improves your ability to study. You will find that your body actually anticipates the demands of studying and prepares for it. Make your study time a treat instead of a dreaded job each day.
- Choose a time of day when you are relaxed and there are few interruptions. Trying to study right before or after meal times probably isn't a good idea in most cases. (Most people are a little too relaxed right after a meal.) You will want to pick a time when your surroundings are quiet and you can spend some time hitting the books. This means that you don't want to study during your lunch hour at work. Trying to take care of the kids while you're trying to study probably won't work well either.
- Never study more than two hours. Most research indicates that one hour of study is about all most people can tolerate. Have you ever gone to a seminar where they try to cram as much as possible into the two or

three hours allotted? What happens after about an hour; people start leaving for places unknown or fidget in their seats. As a person spends more time in study, their attention slowly drifts to other topics and finally away from the area they want to study. If you really want to study more than two hours, make sure you take plenty of breaks. One way to extend your study time is to study for an hour, take a 15-minute break to relieve the stress, then study for another hour.

- Try varying your study technique. You might try having someone quiz you one night and do some memorization another night. Another way to vary your schedule is to spend the first half hour studying and the second half hour having someone quiz you. Varying your technique can reduce the boredom that naturally occurs as study progresses.

As you can see, planning for your study time is fairly important. It really helps if you can study without fear of interruption or of going to sleep. It also helps if you can maintain the most positive attitude possible; you want to study without getting bored. One technique that helps prevent this is to read or study with a big bowl of popcorn. As you study, munch on the popcorn; the action of moving your hand from the bowl to your mouth will stimulate your other muscles just enough to keep you alert. After all, this is your future livelihood. Why should you work at something that bores you? Give yourself every advantage, pick the times when you are best able to study. Make sure you study long enough, but not too long.

Developing good study habits is also important if you want to pass an exam. You always want to maximize the impact of each study session. This means a lot more than just getting into the right frame of mind or using good study practices. It means that you take the time to create the right study environment and to converse with your peers about the topics that will appear on the test.

Developing good study habits

There are many ways to help improve your study time. Some methods work for some people, some for others. Everyone is different. You need to develop a set of study habits that works for you. The best idea is to analyze both your successes and failures to determine what works and what doesn't. The following hints will help you develop a study strategy that maximizes the effects of your study time.

- Always study your weak areas first, then study the areas you feel more confident about. If you have someone quiz you, make sure they quiz you about the weak areas first and the strong areas second. To help determine where your weak areas lie, make sure you look at your notes. If you took the time to take notes about a particular topic, then you are probably weak in that area.

- Have someone quiz you on what you learned. (The instructor will provide you with sample test questions; form your quiz questions using the same format.) Make a game out of studying. Reward yourself with something special if you get a specific number of points toward your goal. You can use the questions you miss as the basis for the next day's study.
- Create a good study environment. Make sure you have a clean desk or table to work at. Reduce any distractions by turning off the radio, closing windows, and asking others in the study area to remain quiet. Adding a good indirect light source and sitting in a comfortable chair can help as well. Make sure you wear comfortable clothing while you study.
- Study the appropriate student guide for the test you want to take. Some people tend to race ahead or look at previously studied areas when they become bored with the current study material. Doing this can actually confuse you rather than help you study. For example, you might find that you start confusing the security rules for NetWare 2.x with those used in NetWare 3.x. Each exam only tests one specific course. Make sure you study for that course. If you find yourself getting bored with the current material, take a short break; get up and move around instead of racing ahead or looking at previously studied material.
- Fill out your notes if you use the outline method of taking notes. Even if you don't you might want to spend part of your study time expanding the notes you took in class. This forces you to remember what the instructor said and what went on during class. It also increases the usefulness of your notes when you need to use them later.
- Spend time discussing the topics you studied in class with your classmates. This allows you to compare notes and ideas about the topics. You might find that someone else has a different viewpoint about what actually took place during class. (The same thing happens when you ask two people about what happened at an accident site; both will see something different.) Talking with your classmates helps you enhance your notes by incorporating their viewpoint as well. It might also help you fill in gaps in your notes. Even the most conscientious person misses things during a discussion.
- If you are a very self-motivated person that tends to rush things, you might rush things and register for an exam before you feel ready to pass it. Even though there is a limited time in which to take all the exams, you don't want to repeat one because you weren't prepared to take it. Make sure you are ready to take the test before you call to register.
- If you tend to procrastinate, you might want to register for your exam immediately after the class is finished. Try setting the date for two weeks from the time your class finishes. This will give you a goal to achieve and enhance your study efforts. Don't let your certificate pass you by; register now for the exam.

As you can see, there are a lot of ways to improve your chances of passing an exam. These include creating and maintaining a positive study environment, reemphasizing important points through quizzes and discussions with your peers, and taking the exam only when you're ready. Following any or all of these suggestions might make the difference between passing the exam and failing it. You might want to take some time to add your own ideas to this list. For example, some people might find that studying outside is more beneficial than studying indoors. Each person is different. The study methods used by one person might not help another. Make sure you optimize your study methods to meet your needs.

Registering for the exam is one of the easiest parts of the process. All you need to do is have a credit card ready and call the Drake testing center. You can register for any test by calling 1-800-RED-EXAM. The person on the other end of the line will ask you a few questions. That's all there is to registering.

Registering for the exam

Of course, there are a few pieces of information you need to know before you can call. You need to know the number of the examination you want to take and the location of your nearest test center. (You can check TABLE 1-1 for a list of exam numbers.) If you don't know the location of the nearest test center, the person registering you can provide a list of locations in your area. They can usually provide you with directions to the test center as well. You might want to drive to the test center from work sometime before the exam so you know how long it takes to get there. This also allows you to test the directions you get and make any required changes. Make sure you add or subtract some time to compensate for differences in traffic flow at the time you plan to travel to the test center. If you make the trip during light traffic, then try it again in heavy traffic.

Make sure you have several exam dates in mind before you call the test center. Otherwise you might find that the test center has filled the date you originally wanted and you have to rush to find another one. Once you get a test date, write it down in several places. Talk to your boss about taking any needed time off well in advance of the test. Make sure you don't schedule other appointments on your test day. Set this day aside for testing and nothing else. (Of course, most people have to go back to work after the exam.)

There are quite a few things people do during the examination; many of them are big time wasters. Some people wander between the drinking fountain and their desk. Others seem more interested in staring at the dots on the wall instead of answering questions. Make sure you use all the time allotted to take the test; don't waste any of it doing other

Taking the exam

activities. Try to maintain your concentration during the entire exam; don't allow interruptions to rob you of the chance to pass. Of course, time isn't the only thing you need to watch during the exam. The following hints should help you take the test faster and improve your chances of passing.

- Look at the time indicator on your screen from time to time, but don't waste time staring at it. Make sure you pace yourself, allotting enough time for each question. You might want to take a quick glance at the time indicator after each question and ignore it the rest of the time.
- Read the entire question. Don't skip over small words like "and" or "not" when reading the question. Small words make a real difference; skipping them could cost you the question. People often miss questions not because they didn't know the answer, but because they failed to read the question fully. Make sure you understand the question before you answer it.
- Read all the answers provided. Sometimes there is more than one correct answer on the screen. You need to pick the most correct answer that you find.
- Remember to put on your Novell hat before you enter the testing area. Novell uses the student manuals as the basis for all the answers in the exam. Even if there is more than one correct way to perform a task, only the Novell way is the correct answer on the exam. In some cases you might see more than one correct Novell answer to a question. Always pick the most complete answer.
- Go with your first instinct. Some people get so psyched out before an exam that they actually overthink the answers. Going with the first answer that comes to mind is correct more often than not, especially if you took the time and effort to study. Don't kill your chances to pass the exam by overthinking the answers.
- Maintain your level of concentration. Even though the exam center administrator tries to provide the very best testing environment possible, there are always distractions that can reduce your concentration level. Concentrate on the test; ignore any outside influences that reduce your level of concentration. You can't perform well on a test that you aren't concentrating on.
- Make sure you take care of your comfort needs before the exam. For example, even though you don't normally eat breakfast, you might want to do so on the day of the exam to boost your energy level. You will also want to wear comfortable clothing. Wear your glasses or contacts so you can see the screen without squinting.

As you can see, the things you notice during the exam are really a matter of how well you prepare before you go into the test center. For example, your body's energy level always affects your concentration level. It's also affected by all the environmental factors under your control, such as the ability to see the screen and wearing comfortable clothing.

Realizing the effects of environmental factors on your mind during an exam is very important. For example, some people go so far as to make out a schedule for the day of the exam. This can help you get from place to place without rushing. Make sure you allow plenty of time to get from place to place. Taking an exam when you feel relaxed is a lot easier than taking one after you have rushed all day. Figure 4-1 shows a typical schedule. Of course, you will need to tailor your schedule for your test needs.

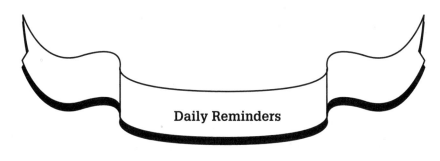

Daily Reminders

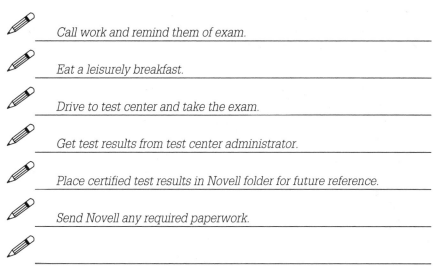

Call work and remind them of exam.

Eat a leisurely breakfast.

Drive to test center and take the exam.

Get test results from test center administrator.

Place certified test results in Novell folder for future reference.

Send Novell any required paperwork.

4-1
Sample exam day reminder list.

Notice that our schedule contains little housekeeping notes like calling work and placing the test results in a folder where you can find them later. These might seem like things you shouldn't have to write down, but writing them down does provide a certain peace of mind while you're taking the exam. You don't need to worry about whether you took care of a specific item because you have all of the things you need to take care of on paper.

What do you do if you fail?

Even if you do fully prepare for an exam, there is still a chance that you will fail it. There is no way for you to take every variable into account to guarantee that you will pass the exam. You might not realize that you have a weak area that the test asks you about. A cold or flu might strike on the day of the exam. An accident might delay you, forcing you to rush to the exam. Any or all of these reasons might prevent you from performing your best on the exam.

How you recover from a failure partially determines how you will react during the next attempt. It can even determine whether you make another attempt to pass the exam. Many people try the exams once, fail, then give up on their certification because the failure is so demoralizing. Remember, certification requires a lot of input from you in the form of dedication and hard work. If certification were an easy task, then the benefits of certification would be a lot less. Don't give up after one attempt to pass an exam.

Understanding the mechanics of failure

Of course nothing is more demoralizing than failing the same test twice. There are several things you should do after failing an exam to make sure it won't happen again. For example, study the areas that gave you the most trouble on the first exam. The following tips will help you pass the exam the second time around. Unlike the other tips in this chapter, these tips usually work for everyone. Make sure you try them all.

- Make a list of the areas where you did well and the areas where you did not. (The test center administrator will provide you with a blank sheet of paper and a pencil you can use for this purpose.) This will tell you where you need to concentrate your study before you take the next exam.
- Maintain a positive attitude. If you convince yourself that you're going to fail, you surely will. Thousands of other people have gotten their certification; there is no reason that you can't get it with the proper training and study. You need to keep this fact in mind while you study for the retake.
- Don't overcompensate by studying too much. Many people make the mistake of punishing themselves for failing by spending hour after hour in front of their desk studying for the next exam. This is probably the worst mistake you can make. While it is important to study for the next exam and find the weak areas that caused you to fail the first time, studying too much can confuse you and cause you to fail again. Make sure you don't study more than two hours per day. (You might want to review the study tips in the previous section of this chapter.)
- Try to remember specific questions that you had trouble with. In fact, you should try to write these down while they're fresh in your memory. Even though it's unlikely you will see these questions on the

next test, they might help you find weak areas in your study strategy. In some cases you might see the same question worded in a different way. This is where reading the question and understanding what it says really helps.

- Always study for a general exam, not the specific exam you took the first time. Trying to study for a specific exam is pointless because each exam contains different questions. Novell writes a new exam from questions in a database for each person that takes an exam. That's why it is so unlikely that you will see the same question again.

Besides the mechanical methods for getting to the next exam, you must deal with the emotional issues as well. Failing an exam always lowers your self-esteem and causes you to doubt your abilities. You need to find outlets for dealing with these emotions. Some people perform some physical activity, such as bowling or tennis, after a failure. The activity helps them release the frustration they feel over failing the exam. Other people work on crafts. A creative endeavor allows them to take their mind off the failure and put it to useful work. Whatever method you use to release the tension of failure, make sure you do it as soon as possible afterward. Don't give yourself time to think about the failure.

Understanding the emotions of failure

You also need to convince yourself that you can pass the exam. Many of the people who start the certification process never complete it because they don't think they can pass the exam. Remember, anyone with reasonable computer skills can pass the exams with the proper training and the right amount of study. A positive attitude is one of your best weapons in passing the exam the next time around. Make sure you maintain a positive attitude as you study and when you take the exam. Keep telling yourself that you can pass the exam.

This chapter provided you with information about the three major areas of taking a test: getting ready for the exam, taking the exam, and recovering from failure. The way that you approach these three areas can greatly affect the final outcome of your certification efforts. After all, the main purpose of going through the course and all the effort of study is to pass the exams. And the only reason you take the exams is to get your certification.

Conclusion

We also looked at what you need to do to register for your exam. This is a fairly easy procedure, but you need to do some advance planning before you call to register. Make sure you give yourself every advantage by taking the exam when you are best prepared to pass it.

5 *Getting the paperwork finished*

The job's never finished until the paperwork's done. This truism applies to Novell certification as well. Even if you finish all the required tests and training, you can still fumble around for several weeks just getting all the paperwork finished. Failure to take care of the paperwork properly won't cost you your certification, but it will cost you time, and as we all know, time is money.

Normally Novell downloads your test scores from the testing center automatically. When you complete all the requirements for your certification, Novell automatically sends you the required paperwork. However, everything doesn't always go as planned. Test results can get lost and hardware failures can trash the test center's files. If any of the test results do get lost, you must provide Novell with documentation proving you passed the required exams and took the required courses.

Of course, the paperwork doesn't end after you submit a few forms to Novell. That's where the work begins. It also includes follow-up calls to make sure that Novell has everything it needs to issue your certificate. You also need to call Novell to make sure that nothing gets lost or overlooked. The bottom line is that you need to maintain a line of communication between yourself and Novell to make sure your certification is issued promptly.

This chapter provides you with step-by-step instructions on filling out the paperwork and getting all the required documentation together. It also tells you which departments you need to talk with and where you need to send the paperwork. Finally, it tells you what kind of paperwork you should get back from Novell and how long it usually takes to receive it.

Getting the paperwork started

It is very important that you begin the paperwork process by getting organized. Make sure you can find the items you need by putting them in one easy-to-find place. Putting all your paperwork in one or two folders is a good idea as well. You might want to create one folder for each course you attend. This way you can keep notes, certificates, and test results for that course in one place. Whatever techniques you use, make sure you keep good records of all the certification items that Novell requires. You want to make it as easy as possible to find this information when you need it during a conversation with a Novell representative.

You should make a list of the paperwork required for your certification. The figures in chapter 1 help you to do this. Make sure you keep this information in your folders as well. If there is a mistake in what you thought was required for certification, then you will want some basis to discuss the mistake with Novell. This might help them improve the level and quality of information that they provide to other candidates in the future. It might also help you get the required exams taken or other certification requirements finished.

How long is too long?

The problem you face now is figuring out when to panic if you don't receive word from Novell regarding your certification. It is always a good idea to take a proactive approach to your certification. Novell downloads data from the test centers about once a week. They compare the information they receive with their current database. If someone passes a test, they add it to their existing record. If Novell can't find your name on its lists, then it adds you to the database as a new applicant. People who complete all their requirements get issued a certificate. A computer performs all these database functions automatically, making the process nearly foolproof. There is very little chance that your examination scores will get lost.

Based on this information, you will want to call Novell about 10 working days after you take your exam to make sure they received the results. Calling Novell ensures that you will receive your certificate on time and that both of your records match. It also reduces the last minute rush you'll experience if you wait until you complete all the requirements to call Novell. You can take care of each mishap as it happens.

Once you complete all your requirements, take time to call Novell again. Make sure you wait the requisite 10 working days after you complete your last requirement. Make sure they have received everything. This is the time to ask the Novell representative how long it will take to receive your certification. Asking this question will let you know when you've waited too long for your certificate to arrive. Always allow a few days after the deadline before you call Novell again. This compensates for slow postal deliveries, especially during the holiday season.

Keeping records is an important part of the certification process. It helps you keep track of where you need to go and what you need to do. Of course, records fulfill an even more important need. Maintaining these paperwork logs might seem like a lot of fuss for nothing, until something gets lost. Chances are good that you won't have any problems, but if you do, the time spent creating these logs will help to resolve any problems or misunderstandings. Make sure you cover all the contingencies by keeping a record of what you do, when you do it, and how you do it. That way you won't have to rely on your memory later when it comes time to figure out what happened. You also want to make sure you maintain good contact with the Novell administration departments without making a nuisance of yourself. Maintaining these logs helps you maintain constant contact without calling too often. Remember, you are the one interested in certification. The Novell representative is only there to help you achieve your goal.

Maintaining a log of the paperwork

The time might arrive when you need to provide Novell with proof that you passed your certification exams. Because proof of requirement completion is your responsibility, it helps to keep a complete log of every certification requirement you complete and when you sent proof of this completion to Novell. You will also want to make notes on what method you used to send the certification material. For example, did you fax the material or send it overnight mail. (If you completed the requirement and simply relied on Novell to download the information from the test center, make sure you record this information as well on the appropriate chapter 1 form. The forms in this chapter are for emergency use only.) Figure 5-1 provides an emergency log you can use for the CNA certification. Figures 5-2 through 5-4 provide the same logs for the CNE, ECNE, and CNI certifications. Use these logs to record any paper correspondence with Novell. For example, if Novell loses your paperwork, you will want to use these forms to record the time, date, and method you used to send them paper copies.

Using the paperwork log

As you can see, each of the forms addresses the needs of only one of the certifications. Using this type of form allows you to make sure you sent everything that Novell needed, as well as keeping track of when and how you sent it. The first few fields of the form contain personal information like your name, the date you started the certification process, and the date you finished it. It includes a list of the requirements you must pass to get the certification. Some of the information needed to fill in the blanks will come from the worksheets you completed in previous chapters. Notice that the course information is blank. This allows you to tailor the form to your specific needs. The course numbers you place in these blanks reflect your operating system specialty. The other fields on this form contain the date you sent proof of passing the requirement to Novell, the method used to send the package, registered mail number (you never want to send this information regular mail), and the date Novell received it. You might even want to include the name of the person who verified that Novell received the package. (This information also appears in the telephone log described in the next paragraph.)

5-1
CNA paperwork log.

Name: _____

Date started: _____   Date completed: _____

Requirement	Course number	Date sent	Method of mailing	Register number	Date received
Submit test results	_____	_____	_____	_____	_____

Name: _____

Date started: _____   Date completed: _____

Requirement	Course number	Date sent	Method of mailing	Register number	Date received
DOS/Microcomputer Concepts	_____	_____	_____	_____	_____
NetWare Service and Support	_____	_____	_____	_____	_____
NetWorking Technologies	_____	_____	_____	_____	_____
System Manager	_____	_____	_____	_____	_____
Advanced System Manager	_____	_____	_____	_____	_____
Elective Credit 1	_____	_____	_____	_____	_____
Elective Credit 2	_____	_____	_____	_____	_____
Elective Credit 3	_____	_____	_____	_____	_____
Elective Credit 4	_____	_____	_____	_____	_____
Elective Credit 5	_____	_____	_____	_____	_____

5-2   *CNE paperwork log.*

Name: _____

Date started: _____   Date completed: _____

Requirement	Course number	Date sent	Method of mailing	Register number	Date received
System Manager	_____	_____	_____	_____	_____
Advanced System Manager	_____	_____	_____	_____	_____
Elective Credit 1	_____	_____	_____	_____	_____
Elective Credit 2	_____	_____	_____	_____	_____
Elective Credit 3	_____	_____	_____	_____	_____
Elective Credit 4	_____	_____	_____	_____	_____
Elective Credit 5	_____	_____	_____	_____	_____
Elective Credit 6	_____	_____	_____	_____	_____
Elective Credit 7	_____	_____	_____	_____	_____

5-3   *ECNE paperwork log.*

Name: _____

Date started: _____   Date completed: _____

Requirement	Course number	Date sent	Method of mailing	Register number	Date received
DOS/Microcomputer Concepts	_____	_____	_____	_____	_____
Product Information	_____	_____	_____	_____	_____
NetWare 2.2 System Manager	_____	_____	_____	_____	_____
NetWare 2.2 Advanced System Manager	_____	_____	_____	_____	_____
NetWare 3.11 System Manager	_____	_____	_____	_____	_____
NetWare 3.11 OS Features Review (optional)	_____	_____	_____	_____	_____
NetWare 3.11 to 4.0 Update (Optional)	_____	_____	_____	_____	_____
NetWare 4.0 System Administration (optional)	_____	_____	_____	_____	_____

5-4   *CNI paperwork log.*

5-4 *Continued.*

Requirement	Course number	Date sent	Method of mailing	Register number	Date received
NetWare Service and Support (category II only)	_____	_____	_____	_____	_____
Networking Technologies (category II only)	_____	_____	_____	_____	_____
NetWare 3.11 Advanced System Manager (category II only)	_____	_____	_____	_____	_____
NetWare 4.0 Advanced Administration (category II only)	_____	_____	_____	_____	_____
NetWare 4.0 Installation Workshop (category II only)	_____	_____	_____	_____	_____
Specialty Course 1	_____	_____	_____	_____	_____
Specialty Course 2	_____	_____	_____	_____	_____
Specialty Course 3	_____	_____	_____	_____	_____
Specialty Course 4	_____	_____	_____	_____	_____
Specialty Course 5	_____	_____	_____	_____	_____

One good alternative to using mail service is faxing your information to Novell. You might want to consider this alternative whenever possible. It is much faster than using the mail and you can call Novell immediately after you send it to make sure they received it. Make sure you call and verify that you have the correct fax number and alert them that you plan to send the information immediately. Once you send the information to Novell, verify that someone at the other end of the fax line received the material in good condition. If they did not receive the information in good condition, resend it right away.

Using the phone log

There is at least one other log you should consider maintaining. This is a record of telephone conversations with the people at Novell. Make sure you record when you call, whom you talked to, pertinent facts about the conversation, and a few notes about what transpired. Figure 5-5 provides a sample telephone log.

Date: _____ Time: _____ Contact person: _____

Phone number: _____ Ext.: _____

Topic: _____

Notes: _____

_____

_____

Problem: _____

_____

Resolution: _____

_____

_____

Date: _____ Time: _____ Contact person: _____

Phone number: _____ Ext.: _____

Topic: _____

Notes: _____

_____

_____

_____

Problem: _____

_____

Resolution: _____

_____

_____

This log file contains enough space for two entries per page. You might want to make a few copies of this sheet to keep on hand for easy reference. Maintaining the log on your computer will allow you to scan the records quickly during a telephone conversation. It also helps you ensure that no information gets overlooked while you talk with the Novell representative. This also makes it a lot faster and easier to maintain your logs and to make sure you haven't forgotten to take care of anything you talked about on the phone or through the mail. Some database managers, such as AskSam or Folio Views, will allow you to enter this type of free-form information quickly. When you need to search for a particular topic, these database managers can search for phrases or whatever else you can remember about the conversation.

Notice that the telephone log contains space for the date, time, and contact person's name. These items are pretty self-explanatory. You will want to include the person's telephone number and extension in the Phone number and Ext. fields of the form.

The Notes field allows you to maintain a record of what each party said during the conversation. Reserve this section for conversation of a general nature. Be specific when taking notes. The more information that you can include the better your chances of resolving any difficulties. Make sure that you record times, dates, phone numbers, and any names mentioned. If there were any commitments made by either party, be sure to make note of it as well. After you finish your conversation with the other person, summarize the conversation from your notes before hanging up. This will help to prevent any miscommunications.

If you called about a problem, make sure you record it in the Problem field of the form. Use descriptive terms for this field. Don't write something like, "Lost package in the mail." Provide yourself with exact details by writing, "Lost copy of the Advanced System Manager exam results in the mail." At least this tells you what test was lost. In addition to this information, you might want to record the registration number and other important facts. If the field does not provide enough room to record all the pertinent information, at least make a note about where you can find the information.

Record the resolution that you and the Novell representative talk about in the Resolution field. Again, document as much of the conversation as possible immediately after the conversation. If you wait very long before documenting your conversation, you might forget something. You can use the contents of the Resolution field to help make a "to do" list later. Creating a "to do" list ensures that you won't forget to follow through on your certification requirements. It also helps you remember when you need to call Novell to recheck the results of a problem resolution.

Filling out the paperwork

There are two sets of paperwork requirements. The standard set applies to anyone who wants to obtain any of the certificates. The CNI set applies only to people who want to become CNIs. The following paragraphs explain these requirements in detail.

The paperwork required for certification by Novell is very minimal. Besides test scores, it consists of a release form and a picture ID request. (Remember, you are responsible for maintaining a copy of your test scores.) As you complete and pass each test, the test center sends a copy of your test scores to Novell. The people in certification administration will then enter that information into a database. If you are just starting the certification process, Novell adds your name and records to the database. As you take each test Novell adds that information to your name. Once you complete all the exams, Novell automatically registers your certification. This applies to all the certification goals: CNA, CNE, and ECNE.

Standard paperwork requirements

The paperwork for the picture ID instructs you about the specifications for the photograph. The picture ID is proof of your certification. In most cases you can get this picture taken at any studio that specializes in passport or visa photographs. While color pictures are nice, Novell does not require that you provide one. Black-and-white photographs work fine for your identification card. Make sure that you provide Novell with the best picture you get. The photo studio will normally take four pictures, unless you request more. You might also want to dress in your normal work clothes and wear anything you normally wear on the job (like glasses).

The paperwork required for the CNI is just about the same as for the other certifications. The only real difference is the initial application and having to send Novell a copy of your course certificates. Remember that to become a CNI you must attend each of the classes that Novell certifies you to teach. After completing the courses, call the CNI administration department and tell them that you completed all your courses. They will then want you to send them a copy of the course certification for each class. This can be faxed or mailed, and you should include a cover page with your name, address, phone number, and why you are sending the certificate copies. Make sure you take the extra step of sending your certificates by fax or registered mail. Never send the original certificate; always send a copy. After you complete this step you are ready to take the CNI competency exams.

CNI paperwork requirements

Once you complete the competency exams you will need to attend the Train the Trainer (TTT) class. You must call Novell to register for the class. If you have not completed the exams you will not be able to attend the TTT class. You should make sure that all your test scores and passing dates are on your paperwork log form. After registering for the TTT class, Novell will send you a confirmation letter with the class dates, times, location, lodging information, and directions. Keep this information in your paperwork folder until the date of the class.

On the first day you attend class, make sure you have the confirmation letter in case you have any problems or mix-ups. After completing the TTT course, you will want to retain this letter with your other paperwork for any future reference. Upon completion of the your TTT class Novell will send you a letter stating whether you passed the class or not. You will want to retain this letter with your other documents as well.

If you were successful in completing the TTT class you will be eligible to teach the appropriate classes. At the end of each year Novell sends you a recertification invoice. Novell applies the fee towards updating your manuals and provides you with the education bulletins and Application Notes. Again, you will want to retain a copy of this invoice with your records.

Checking on the paperwork

Even though Novell will automatically register your certification, it is your responsibility to follow up. You can never take too many precautions when it comes to your certification. After all, you have just spent many hours and dollars to get this far. The last thing you want now is to have some lost or misplaced paperwork hold up your certification or, worse yet, cause you to have to retake a test. After completing your last test, give Novell about 7 to 10 working days to process the paperwork. After that time, call the certification administration to check the status of your certification. The people in the administration department are very courteous and helpful when you call. Chances are very good that Novell has already processed your certification and it is on its way to you. If Novell has not processed the paperwork yet, then you can inform them of your standing and they can start the process moving.

Make sure you're armed with all the information you need to talk intelligently with the Novell representative before you call. This includes your logs and the actual documentation. The more information that you can give the Novell representative, the faster and more accurately Novell can take care of your paperwork.

When you call into the Novell CNA/CNE/CNI administration, make sure you have a list of any important telephone numbers as well. For example, make sure you have a fax number that Novell can use to send you any required information if necessary.

Victory— getting your certificate

The day of victory is the day your certificate finally arrives in the mail. Your certificate will arrive in your "welcome aboard" kit from Novell. There is nothing like the sense of accomplishment you will feel when you finally get to see the certificate you worked so long to get. This is a time when you need to spend a little time with your new credentials.

Make sure Novell filled in your name and other important information areas on your certificate correctly. You might want to write down some of the vital information like your CNA/CNE/ECNE/CNI number as well. You can provide this number to your clients or potential employers for verification purposes.

The kit contains many other items besides the certification certificate. It includes your Network Support Encyclopedia (covered in chapter 7) and some other paperwork. This paperwork includes a release form granting Novell permission to publish your name in the appropriate section of NetWire. Another form instructs you to send a passport-style photo of yourself to Novell. The photograph is placed on your ID badge and then sent back to you. Once you receive your ID badge, display it to your customers or employers as proof of certification. Chapter 6 tells you how to use your new badge when you want to work for someone else. Chapter 8 covers the use and purpose of the badge when you use it as a consultant.

You will also want to take time to get your certification logo put on any brochures or sales literature. If you aren't a consultant or in the retail business, you might want to put your logo somewhere on your resume. This might attract the attention of a future employer. You might also want to make some photocopies of the certificate and include it at the end of your resume. Whatever situation you find yourself in, make sure you let everyone know that you finally achieved your goal of getting your certification. After all, you shared your dreams of certification with them. They supported you throughout the courses, long hours of studying, and the testing process. This includes not only telling your friends, family and coworkers, but also framing your certificate and displaying it. Many companies and resellers will use your certification to add credibility to their organization. This is an important part of making your certification work for you.

Conclusion

This chapter helped you through the paperwork process required to get your certification. It began with a few simple ideas on ways to get the paperwork started and included some pointers on making sure that Novell actually receives your paperwork. It also provided a few tips on ensuring you have all the required paperwork together before you mail the package.

The next section of the chapter looked at some of the paperwork you need to maintain. It's important to maintain a log of the work you submit to Novell. This way you have a ready list to refer to when you call Novell to request the status of your certification. You can provide the dates when you shipped things to Novell and tell them how the package was shipped. This might help you to locate items that get lost.

We also looked at the actual process of filling out the paperwork. Just like with other forms, filling out your certification forms is very important. You must do it correctly if you expect to get your certification.

Finally, we looked at the communication process between you and Novell. It's important to verify that Novell receives all the paperwork you send for their approval. You need to maintain a line of communication to make it easy for someone to contact you regarding your certification.

The last section of this chapter dealt with actually receiving your certification. After all the testing and paperwork, it's nice to see that certificate hanging on the wall. A Novell certification is more than just a sheepskin; it's verification of your ability to administrate or install networks. It tells the world that you have gained the level of knowledge required to make their network a joy to use.

6 *Using your certification to your advantage*

Have you ever seen someone who had all the advantages lose out to someone else because they didn't know how to use what they had? It happens all the time in the movies. We find ourselves cheering for the underdog as he or she overcomes the resources of some villain to win in the end. Of course, the movies don't truly reflect real life. In real life the consequences of not using an advantage are not nearly so entertaining; in fact, they can be downright devastating. Imagine losing a job you really wanted to someone less qualified than you, simply because you didn't market your skills properly. Gaining access to a skill is only the first step in using it as a career-enhancing tool. You must learn to use this skill to your advantage in the marketplace.

Introduction

As you can see, the trick to gaining the full benefit of your certification comes from marketing your skills to a potential employer. This chapter helps you understand what you need to do to use the certification you acquire to your benefit. This particular chapter focuses on the individual working for someone else. It covers a number of topics from advancing in your current company to getting a new (and hopefully better) job based on your training. (See chapter 8 for information on how consultants can use their Novell certification to good advantage in the marketplace.)

Two main methods of enhancing your career are covered in this chapter. Either method will help you gain the full benefit of obtaining your certification, but each uses entirely different approaches. Section one covers the possibility of advancing within your own company. This is the route that will appeal to people who are happy with their current company. Many people are very happy with their jobs. If you fall into this category, there is absolutely no reason to move to a new company.

There is another group of people who only take a job for the short term until they can get something better. (In fact, some employers hire people knowing that they don't intend to stay.) Moving from one company to another can help you gain the recognition you need in addition to improved company benefits. If you want to make a change from your current company, then it pays to follow the two-step plan outlined in section two. The first step is preparing your resume. The second step is making the best possible impression during an interview.

Advancing within your current company

There are a lot of ways to advance within your current company. Your boss might get promoted or leave for another company. If you demonstrate the abilities required to take over that position, then your company might choose to promote you. Another method of advancing is to create your own position. Your company might want to get rid of an old method of doing something and replace it with a newer, more efficient method. If you provide your company with enough reason to make the change, you might find yourself in charge of the group responsible for implementing the change. After the change is finished, you could find yourself in an entirely new position as head of the group. Some companies will simply change your job title to match the work that you're doing. In some cases this includes additional pay or other benefits. Whatever method you choose to follow, you need to create an advancement plan. Don't wait for opportunity to knock because it seldom does. Create your own opportunities within the workplace.

The fact that your company chose to pay for your certification shows that there is an advancement opportunity waiting for you when you return. Even if your company already has a network in place, there is some reason for them to train you. Your first goal in getting a promotion or new position is to find out why you are getting the training. Use this reason as the basis for your advancement plan. Of course this is only the beginning. You might find that you have to do a lot of detective work before you work out an advancement plan. Management often treats new network installations or the departure of a manager as a closely guarded secret. Finding out what plans your company has could help you prepare for the future. The following tips should help you formulate some advancement goals and strategies.

- If your company already has a network, try to find out if anyone from that section is leaving the company. You might find that you will eventually fill their position if you demonstrate the proper skills to the company. Make sure you concentrate on ways of enhancing these skills.

- Check to see if your company is increasing the size of the network or installing a new network. If they are installing a new network, you might be chosen to maintain it. An expanding network could show that you are at least in line for a title change.
- Find out if your company is creating a new workgroup. Some companies create splinter organizations when they want to introduce a new product or when the current group becomes too large. If there are no plans to expand the current network, then your company might want to create such a splinter group. You could become the network administrator for the new workgroup.
- See if your company recently won a large contract. A company might create a small workgroup to deal with a specific contract. If so, your new position might only last the term of the contract. Figuring out ways to make this new position permanent is a very important consideration. You need to consider the longevity of any advancement or title change you get.

Of course, some employers won't recognize your new status unless you bring it to their attention. There are some situations where you might find that your certification is more of a handicap than an asset. Take whatever steps are needed to prevent this situation from happening. In most cases your employer will not want to lose the investment in time and money that the company made to get you certified. You can use this as leverage when you try to correct these problem situations. The following paragraphs list some of the problems you might experience.

- In some cases a company will help you get your certification and promise you the sun, moon, and stars until you achieve your goal. As soon as you get back to work, you find that instead of a promotion you get more work instead. Your company might feel perfectly justified in forcing you to perform all your previous tasks in addition to the new network administration tasks. Don't let this happen. If your company promises you anything to get your new certification, make sure you get the promises in writing. Verbal promises last only as long as you can hear the words.
- The company might ask you to sign a contract promising that you will work for them a specific amount of time after you receive your certification. They might also ask you to sign a document promising to pay back the cost of certification if you fail to obtain it. Make sure you get some concessions from the company in exchange for these guarantees. Never give your company something for nothing. In many

states it is illegal to hold you to such a contract or make you pay the employer back for education.
- You might find that the level of cooperation drops drastically once you complete a network installation. Without the proper tools and support, you will never maintain the network in peak operating condition. Make sure you talk to the company about these problems in advance. Don't make your new certification a source of problems.

Now that you have some ideas about the positive and negative aspects of getting a certification, you can formulate an advancement plan. As the previous paragraphs showed, there are at least three different ways of getting a promotion within a company. The following paragraphs examine these three methods of advancing within your company. Of course, there are probably many other ways that you can pursue advancement. These methods simply provide ideas that you can use to create your own advancement plan.

Promotion   Many people start at a particular company and stay there for their entire working career. They wait for the person ahead of them to either get a promotion or leave the company. As new positions open, these people try to fill them before someone else does. This is a perfectly good way to advance your career. There are several different ways that you can enhance your chances of getting that new position based on your new certification and the longevity of your relationship with the company.

- You can demonstrate an extensive knowledge of the company's way of doing things. This translates into a network administrator who is familiar with company policies. It means that you can do the job faster and more efficiently than someone hired from outside of the company.
- Longevity also translates into a knowledge of the people working at the company. You probably have a good idea of who is working at the company, how long they have worked there, what their job responsibilities are, and what you can do to help them. All of this knowledge means that you will spend less time getting the network set up and maintaining it. It also means that you will probably make fewer mistakes.
- The fact that you have held several positions in the same company means that you can better identify with problem areas within the company. You have a greater understanding of why certain policies are in place and what each person needs to do their work because you have done their job in the past.
- The Novell certification you receive opens new doors of responsibility. Your past job performance will help you get an advancement based on positive proof that you can handle added responsibility. Everyone in the company knows you are capable of doing the job. They don't have to

rely on the second-hand information provided by someone you worked for in the past.

As you can see, the means of getting a promotion once a door of opportunity opens is there. Of course, simply because the door opens does not mean that management will put you in the new position. You must earn the new position. As a result, there are other things you need to do as well. For one thing, you can't advance if you don't know where all the windows of opportunity exist. Figure 6-1 shows a typical company organizational chart.

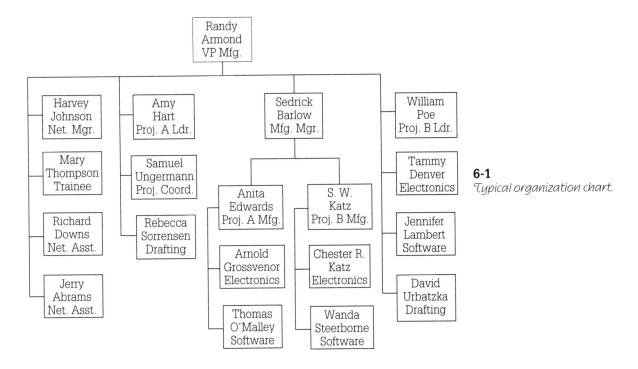

6-1
Typical organization chart.

If you are Mary Thompson on the chart, the first thing you might think is that your next promotion opportunity is limited to Harvey Johnson's job. But in reality many other windows of opportunity are just waiting for you. For example, as you help administer the network you will find out about the tasks performed by Amy Hart or William Poe. You might even set your sights higher by trying for the position held by Sedrick Barlow. Of course, your ultimate goal might include the vice president's job. The important thing to remember is the organization of your company; look for opportunities to advance yourself. You might even want to get a copy of your company's organizational chart (or make one of your own).

So how does this relate back to your certification? Remember, there are many ways to use your certification as a key to future promotions. Don't limit your thinking to a single area or one possible means of using it. You can use the information you obtain from administering the network to prove your worth in other areas of the company as well. Companies look for people who are willing to take charge, that show a real involvement in their work. They won't promote someone who simply does their work.

Now it's time to combine everything you learned from the preceding paragraphs into a plan of attack. The various pieces of information discussed should provide you with all you need to know to fill out the advancement form in FIG. 6-2. Notice that this form is specially designed for someone who wants to use the advancement route to improve their position in the company.

The form begins with a little self-examination. It asks you to provide your current position and salary. This gives you a starting point; it shows where you are now. You need a starting point to see how far you progress toward your goal. The next two sections of the form provide places for two goals. These are the positions you want to target as potential places for advancement. Make sure you pick realistic goals or you will find disappointment rather than advancement. Picking two goals is an essential part of the planning process. You must maximize your chances of advancing in the company. As a result, you must always look at more than one place for an advancement opportunity.

There are four sections in each goals section. The first section asks you to define the goal itself. Make sure you include the title, pay, and any responsibility you would like to take as part of the advancement. The next thing you need to do is relate your networking experience to the position you want to attain. This serves as a reality check. It asks you to determine how you can use the experience you gain now to help in later promotions. The third area asks you to decide what other experience you need to get to the next position. This is an important consideration because it helps you to see opportunities to gain needed experience. For example, when the boss asks for volunteers for a project, it is really an opportunity to grab some experience. Finally, the fourth section asks you to determine what educational requirements the new position requires. Management is interested in both knowledge and experience. Don't let someone fresh from college take your position from you. Make sure you prepare for both areas.

One final piece of advice for the person who wants to advance in their current company. You need to grab opportunities because they seldom knock very loud. Look for opportunities to gain experience and show management that you are ready for a promotion. Always think about the possibilities; don't stoop to reactive attempts at advancement. The

Date: _____ Current job title: _____

Current pay rate: _____ Target pay rate: _____

Advancement goal 1: _____

Date of anticipated advance: _____

How will your networking experience help you attain your goal? _____

_____

_____

Experience needed to attain goal: _____

_____

Education needed to attain goal: _____

6-2
*Advancement through
promotion worksheet.*

_____

Advancement goal 2: _____

Date of anticipated advance: _____

How will your networking experience help you attain your goal? _____

_____

_____

Experience needed to attain goal: _____

_____

Education needed to attain goal: _____

_____

proactive approach always yields some result; the reactive approach always yields stagnation. Of course, you need to think about the consequences of your plan before you present it. A proactive approach can have negative as well as positive results. Make sure you find the opportunities that yield positive results.

Some people still possess the frontier spirit. They go where no one else will go and do the things that no one ever thought about doing. Inventors

**Creating a
new position**

and scientists commonly fall into this category. However, this same set of skills can work to your benefit in the corporate environment as well. Many people have made fortunes by inventing a position and showing management that the company can't survive without it. This is where the network administrator is today. You have an opportunity to break new ground, to create your own position. The network administrator is truly at the forefront of technology.

Of course, the network administrator doesn't always start with many benefits and has even less recognition. Sometimes a network administrator starts as a grunt laborer under someone who doesn't appear to understand what the company needs and has no desire to learn. Instead of forcing yourself to endure untold hardship under someone who cares little about what you do, turn the situation around. Look at this situation as an opportunity to create a new position. If you can show management that you can produce better results without your current boss standing over your head, you might find that you can create your own position. Of course, in many cases, the payment for failure to convince management of the benefits of the new position is dismissal. (At the very least, your old boss will never trust you again.)

As you can see, this method of advancement is not without risks. But the risks are worth it to someone prepared to take advantage of the results. Creating your own position means that you control how your job takes shape. It also means that your chances of getting promoted to upper management are much better. If you prove that you are an idea person, someone capable of thinking on their own, management might sit up and take notice.

So how do you start planning for a new position? Everything requires planning. You must take time to create a proposal that demonstrates the company needs the new position you want to create. More than that, you must demonstrate that you are the best candidate for the position. Just because you prove the company needs a new position doesn't mean you'll get it. You must prove that you are the only person for the job, both through qualifications and in repayment to the company. Figure 6-3 shows a sample of what you can do to start the planning process.

There are several interesting features on this form. The first section states a starting and ending date to accomplish your goal. Make sure you enter both dates to give yourself a target to reach. Procrastination is the worst thing you can do to your plans for creating a new position. Don't be afraid to change the ending date if necessary; you'll want to prepare the best presentation possible. The next section talks about the position itself. It is very important to define a potential title name, why the position is important, to conceptualize any potential costs and problems associated with creating the position, and to provide management with a projected payback period for their investment. Make sure you list both tangible and intangible benefits. In most cases you will want to create a position that provides a payback in both areas to the company. The third section states why you are the person to fill this position. You must write these reasons down and back them up with good arguments. Make sure you demonstrate beyond a shadow of a doubt that you are the person to fill the position. The final area is a checklist of items you need to complete before you make your presentation. This worksheet is for your benefit; the other items provide information to management in an easy-to-understand manner. If you can't express your idea to management, there is no reason to believe they will create the new position for you.

Current date: _____ Planned presentation date: _____

New position title: _____

Reason the new position is important: _____

_____

_____

_____

_____

Cost of creating the position: _____

Potential cost benefit: _____ Payback time: _____

Intangible benefits: _____

_____

_____

Reasons you should take the new position: _____

_____

_____

❑ Cost Analysis   ❑ Full Presentation

❑ Time Analysis   ❑ Handouts

❑ Benefits Analysis   ❑ Graphs and Charts

❑ Requirements for the Position ❑ Presentation Scheduled

6-3
Sample plan for creating your own position.

Now it's time to look at some of those additional pieces of information presented on the form. The first item is a cost analysis. You will want to create a full cost analysis showing exactly what it will cost the company to create the new position you propose. At the very least it will cost the company a pay raise. (Hopefully you are not going through all this work for the sheer gratification of doing the work.) Make sure you look for hidden costs as well. Consider items like additional staff and equipment. Make sure you show how the company can amortize this investment over a period of time. Any friends you gain in accounting can probably help you in this area.

The next thing you want to do is create a time analysis. As a minimum you need to create a milestone chart with goals that you expect to meet by specific dates. Some of the more advanced project management programs could help you in this regard. You might find a computer with one of these programs in the engineering or manufacturing area of your company. Ask the supervisor if you can use the program. (You might need to come in after working hours to perform this work.) Of course, you can even use a standard drawing program to create the charts you need, but project management software will help you look for potential scheduling conflicts. Project management software will also make it easy to incorporate changes to your plan.

The benefits analysis is one of the most important parts of your presentation. Management tends to focus on the negative element of any form of change: the cost of making it. You need to focus their attention on the positive elements of what they will obtain from the change. Make sure you look at the company's interests when you write the list of benefits, not the elements that are attractive to you. For example, while you might find the increased responsibility interesting, management won't. However, they will find increased revenues or other company-related benefits interesting.

Provide management with a complete listing of all the requirements for the position. This accomplishes two purposes. First, it defines the position and shows management that you took the time to think this idea through. It also helps you define your position later. One of the reasons that some new position ideas fail is that they are ill-defined at the very start. Some people actually make their jobs more difficult by not defining what they mean at the start of a project. This leaves the door for interpretation open. Second, you can use the requirements as part of your arguments later. For example, you can use the requirements to show management that you are the only person who can perform the job adequately. Make all the pieces of your presentation fit together into a well-coordinated plan.

Create a full presentation for management. Include slides, graphs, charts, handouts, and anything else you can think of to make the presentation interesting. Remember, you are trying to sell an idea that many people in management will want to resist. This is not a situation where you are starting with an open-minded audience; you have to open their minds to the potential benefits of the new position.

Handouts really help keep people interested if you use them correctly. There are several rules you need to observe during the presentation. For example, have someone help you with this element of your presentation. Don't make the mistake of providing management with all your handouts at once. Give them out as management needs to look at them. Otherwise you might find that you lose your audience to the handouts that were supposed to keep them interested in your presentation. They will skim through them trying to find the bottom line and not get the full picture that you are presenting to them. You should also refer to your handouts frequently during the presentation. Otherwise, management will wonder why you took the time to prepare them.

Graphs and charts are an extremely important part of your presentation. Studies show that people can absorb information in graphic form much better and faster than they can in printed form. The printed material is abstract; the graphic form is a lot more concrete. Rather than burden management with a lot of tabular data, present it in graphic form and offer to allow them to see the tables later. Make sure you make the actual data available, but keep your presentation interesting by using graphics.

You need to schedule your presentation. Make sure you get a specific date from management. A common problem is that management will say they want to see your presentation "sometime soon." They keep putting the presentation off until (hopefully) you forget about showing it to them. To get their approval you might need to tell them about some aspects of your idea. Get management as excited as you are about this new position. Make sure you don't tell them everything; keep some surprises for the meeting itself. Schedule a conference room for the meeting. Avoid presenting your idea in someone's office. Reduce the chances of political posturing by holding the meeting in a neutral setting. Doing so can help alleviate the problem of trying to answer questions from someone who only asks them to increase his or her political stature in the company. In addition, holding the meeting in a conference room reduces the risk of interruptions such as phone calls and other people walking in. Get everything ready for the meeting well in advance. Don't wait until the last minute.

As you can see, creating a successful presentation is a challenge in many ways. You need to do a lot of preparation before you will be able to present your idea to management. Take the time to research your company thoroughly. Make sure you can tell management everything they need to know about your idea. Show them that you did your homework, that you're interested enough in the company to devote the time required to find out about it. You might want to spend some time viewing presentations made by other people in the company as well. Notice the ideas and presentation methods that seem to attract the attention of key management personnel. These methods usually guarantee some measure of success when you make your presentation. Make sure you write these ideas down to use in your presentation.

Of course, there are several ways you can use your certification to attain your goals. For one thing, as network administrator you will meet many of the people you need to influence. This personal contact can make the difference between getting the new position approved and looking for a new job. Make sure you take the personalties of the individual members of management into account as you prepare your presentation.

You can also use your position to obtain information about the company and its operations. As network administrator you will gain access to many areas of the company that other people might not see. You will see the broad view of all the jobs the people in the company perform. Your position will expose you to all the products the company makes and gives you inside information about how these products could improve. The possibilities for gaining knowledge are almost unlimited.

Finally, your position as network administrator will give you a unique view of both management and employees. You can use this view to provide unique insights as you present your ideas to management. Present some of the employee needs from a management viewpoint during your presentation.

Title change   There are those people in any company that don't really want to advance into management. They are happy working at their current position and don't really want the added responsibility that a promotion brings. This is not necessarily bad. Someone has to fill these positions and if you're happy working there, then a management post might not provide the type of work environment you want.

Of course, you still want some form of recognition for your achievement. After all, you did go through all the effort required to get your certification and you want management to recognize that achievement. One of the best ways to get recognition is to provide management with a reason to change your title. You'll work for the same boss at the same pay doing about the same work, but the title change will show that you have made some type of change in your qualifications. Of course, a title change could lead to some additional pay as well.

So what do you do to get this title change? First, you could simply schedule a meeting with your boss and ask for the change. You might be surprised to find that your boss will help you get a title change with no additional effort on your part. (You might have to shuffle some paperwork, but this is really a very minor consideration.)

If this first approach doesn't work, put your request in writing. Make sure you state some reasons why the title change is so important. It will give your boss an incentive to tell you why he or she won't consider a title change. It will also provide your boss with something that can be passed up to his or her superior. The reason that your boss didn't provide the title change could involve a lack of authority to do so. The following paragraphs provide some ideas on arguments you can use to get a title change.

- Because your job tasks have changed since you got your Novell certification, why not a title change to go along with it? Changes in job tasks should show up in your job title as well.
- A new job title will help distinguish between the tasks you perform and those performed by other employees.
- A new job title is a lot less expensive than a raise. (Of course, you can always argue later that your new title entitles you to a pay raise.)
- A new job title could potentially add to the company's prestige by showing they have an up-to-date networking system specialist. You need to add some arguments that show whom this would affect.
- Providing you with a new job title could enhance the way management views your boss's position. It would show that he or she had a wider area of responsibility than before.

Of course, these are just a few of the arguments you can use to convince your boss to grant you a new job title. The important thing is that you deserve the new title. If your current title is administrative assistant, it hardly reflects your new position as a network administrator. Even if you perform this job on a part-time basis, your job title should reflect your change in status.

A job title change can help you in the future in several ways, even if it doesn't appear to help you today. First, if you do decide to go to another company, the title change will appear as a promotion. There is no way your future employer will know that you didn't receive any additional benefits for the change in title unless you tell them. Second, it could help you get better raises in your current company. If you demonstrate an increased level of knowledge, then many companies are willing to pay for that increased knowledge. The only problem is that upper management will never know that your status has changed unless you get it down on paper somewhere. A change in title is one of the most efficient and most noticeable methods of doing so.

Getting a title change might not seem very exciting. In fact, it might seem as if you accomplished nothing at all. Of course, nothing is further from the truth. A title change might not dramatically affect your career today, but it could help a great deal in the future. Even if you don't want to get into management in your current company, it is very important that you gain the recognition you deserve for getting your Novell certification.

Moving to a different company

Some people work at a company to gain experience and a specific level of education, then move to another company. The reason for this strategy is quite simple; you can advance a lot faster using this technique than you can by staying at your current company. Of course, you give up quite a bit when you use this strategy. For example, many companies will not provide you with any kind of retirement unless you stay for a specific number of years (anywhere from 10 to 20 years). There are other benefits that companies offer as well. For example, in some companies you share in the stock program after you work there for five years. If you move from company to company in pursuit of a better position, you might never meet this requirement.

Once you weigh the consequences of moving around and decide that you want to improve your position more than you want to gain these other benefits, you need to consider how to present yourself to a potential employer. This includes both a written and a verbal presentation. The written presentation is commonly called a resume, while the verbal presentation is called an interview. The following paragraphs show you how to leverage your Novell certification as part of both processes.

Getting your resume together

Getting any resume together includes three steps. First, you need to research the company that you want to work for. (You might want to research several companies to improve your chances of getting a job.) You can get information about a company in several ways. The annual report is always a good source of information. It tells you about the company's stability and what products it makes. The annual report will also tell you a little about the management of the company. Talking with employees of the company is useful, but not always easy to do. It takes time to make friends with someone who works at a company you want to work for, but you can accomplish it. An employee can tell you about the real working conditions within the company and might put you in contact with the person you need to contact with a resume later. Look through the newspaper as well. Larger companies usually appear in the newspaper from time-to-time. Use this free source of information as much as possible.

Once you finish your research, you need to use that information to write a convincing cover letter for your resume. The cover letter should never take more than one (or perhaps two) pages. You need to show your potential employer that you're a skilled professional. Make sure you mention your Novell certification. The letter also needs to show that you've researched the company. Try to tie your skills into company needs. You need to convince the company that they require your services.

Finally, write your resume. Actually, there are only a few stock styles of resume and you can keep copies of them up to date fairly easily. Some people use one stock style of resume, but this could limit your opportunities to target the resume and letter to the company you want to work for. It almost always pays to take the extra time to tailor your resume to the situation. For one thing, you need to leave out some of your less important qualifications as you gain more experience. What if a potential employer is looking for that skill? Writing a resume for each job you want to apply for is never a waste of time. This is why you want to research the needs of each company.

Of course, there are other things that you need to do to maximize the potential of the letter and resume you write. If you have ever seen the pile of letters and resumes received for a job, you will understand why it is important to differentiate your letter from everyone else's. Some people try to do this with colored envelopes or by using fancy type. All these techniques show the potential employer is that you sent out a form letter, with a form resume, and a standard envelope. However, as a Novell certificate holder you do have one thing that differentiates you from the competition, your logo. Placing the Novell logo on the envelope, the letter, and your resume could make them stand out from the competition. If you get your stationery printed with the logo, then individually print each letter and resume, you'll have a winning combination for getting someone's attention.

The following paragraphs describe the three steps you need to accomplish to write the best resume and cover letter possible. Because these items are your emissaries to a potential employer, it pays to take the time required to prepare them properly. The ideas in these paragraphs should help you attain your goal.

Research the company   Always take time to fully research a company that you want to work for. After all, how do you really know that working for a company will enhance your career until you fully research it? You need to determine what working conditions are like, what types of work you can expect to perform, the advancement potential within the company, and any potential problems you might encounter. It also pays to check into the financial stability of the company. You don't want to work hard to get a job at a company only to get laid off a month later because of a shortage of work. All these considerations are important from a personal perspective.

There are other good reasons to fully research the company. When you go in for your interview, your future boss will probably spend a lot of time telling you about what the company does. Of course, this is a very important part of the interview process. What your boss is really looking at is how much you know about the company. The questions that he or she asks really point to a need to learn how much you know. What can you do for the company? That's the question your potential boss is asking. If you research the company, then you can answer questions of this sort. Showing that you know a lot about the company from an external point of view really helps differentiate you from other job applicants.

As you can see, the research you perform is never wasted. You can use it today to determine if you even want to apply for the job. Tomorrow you can use it to write your cover letter and individualize your resume. Next week you can use it to impress your future boss during the interview. And the research even helps you to acclimate to your new work environment quickly.

Write a convincing cover letter Writing a convincing cover letter is a somewhat daunting task. It takes a lot of time and effort to put a good cover letter together. What goes into a convincing cover letter? The following paragraphs will help you with some ideas that you can incorporate into your cover letter.

- Writing a convincing cover letter does not mean a sentimental plea for a job or that you are begging. After reading several dozen letters that appear to beg for the job a company is offering, it is refreshing to read something straightforward and easy to understand. Make your point clear. You have something of value to offer a potential employer.
- Always keep your sentences short and clear. Make your point, then get onto the next subject. If you don't provide enough information about a particular topic, your future employer will ask about it during the interview. (Of course, too little information is not a good goal either because you might never get that interview.)
- Ask someone else to read your letter and tell you what they think of it. You might be surprised to find out how little information you really conveyed. If a potential employer read the same letter, it would end up in the circular file and you would never get a chance at an interview.

- Use an outline if necessary to focus your ideas. If your cover letter rambles from topic to topic, someone reading it will certainly think you are like that in person. Your letter reflects your personality. Make sure it is an accurate mirror of who you are and what you have to represent.
- Never write more than a one-page letter unless a future employer asks for more information than can fit on one page. Always keep your letters under two pages. No one wants to read 100 five- or six-page letters. If your letter is more than two pages long, it could end up in the circular file. Ideally it should get the point across within a paragraph or two.
- Make sure you express all your ideas in the letter. If your research shows that a potential employer is looking for specific qualifications, you will want to address all these qualifications in your letter and resume. Your letter is the specific part of your presentation, so it should address specific qualifications. Write down a list of these qualifications and check them off as you address them in the letter.
- Avoid writing to "Dear Sir" in your letter. Learn the name and title of the person you're writing to. Any other behavior will seem rude to the person reading your letter. (Especially if your future employer is a woman receiving a letter addressed to "Dear Sir.")
- When writing your cover letter and resume make absolutely certain that all of your spelling, grammar, and punctuation are correct. You can be almost certain it will end up in the rejection pile if there are any errors. Also avoid hand-writing the cover letter and resume. Hand-writing them will make it appear that you threw something together at the last moment. The prospective employer might look at several dozen to several hundred resumes for this position; the hand-written or hard to read letters and resumes have a very slim chance of getting read. A manager will usually throw them away. Using a good word processor, such as Microsoft Word or WordPerfect, will allow you to create a professional, easy-to-read cover letter and resume. If you do not have access to a word processor, invest the money to have a professional service type your letter and resume for you.
- You should also consider the stationery that you use. Flashy stationery will attract the manager's attention. However, the easier your letter is to read, the better the chance of having it read completely. Consider using a color of paper that is soothing on the eyes. The stark white of standard paper with black ink is sometimes very annoying. Consider paper that is off-white, beige, light green, or light blue. These colors go well with black ink, making the letter very easy to read. Never use stationery from your current employer, no matter how much prestige it might carry. This sends a signal to the prospective employer that you misuse company property, company time, and might even steal from the company. Using a current company's stationery might seem like

just a story, but many people do it all the time and then they wonder why they never get an interview.

- Always make sure that you add personal touches to a cover letter. Two ways to accomplish this are to personally sign the cover letter and to mention the recipient's name and company name whenever possible. These add a personal touch and show that this is not just a form letter that you sent out.

As you can see, there is a lot you can do to enhance the quality of your cover letter. Of course, these are only a few ideas. You might even want to consider taking a business writing course at a community college. A course of this type will not only help you write your letter and resume in clear and easy-to-understand language, but will improve your job performance as well. It never hurts to know how to express yourself both verbally and in writing.

Now that you have some ideas about what to include in your letter and how to present it to an employer, it's time to look at an example. Figure 6-4 is an example cover letter.

As you can see, this letter uses the Novell certification label in the lower left corner. This helps to differentiate the letter from others the employer might look at. Notice that there is a lot of white space. The letter does not look cramped or difficult to read. Make your letter as inviting to read as possible. The letter also contains the names and addresses of both parties; this is for your benefit as well as that of your future employer. The first paragraph tells your future employer how you meet the qualifications set by the advertisement. It also tells them where you saw the advertisement. The second paragraph tells the employer why they should consider you before someone else. This is an important part of the cover letter. You have to gain the interest of the person reading the letter or they will never read your resume.

Prepare a resume tailored to your audience   There are several stock resume formats you can use. Any good business writing book will provide you with complete examples of these formats. The two most important formats for someone who is trying to emphasize their Novell certification are those that emphasize experience and education. Use the experience slant if you have more than three years invested in your certification. An employer always looks favorably on someone who has experience as well as education. If you just got your certification, you will want to use the education slant. Show your future employer that you have all the knowledge required to do the work.

So what are the important points of a resume? The following paragraphs provide you with some ideas on how you can leverage your Novell

John Mueller
2020 Twin Palms Street
River City, CA 92104-3703
619-881-7732 business
619-881-7733 fax

9 April 1993

Mary Jones
Engineering Manager
The Industrial Place
3288 The Place Street
Somewhere, CA 92112

Dear Ms. Jones:

I recently saw your advertisement for a CNE in the California Job Times. According to the ad, you need someone with a minimum of two years experience and proof of certification. As you can see from the attached resume, I can meet both qualifications. I worked two years at Jobber Industrial and three years at Technical Stuff, Inc. I can provide my certification papers to you on request. (A copy of the certification is attached to the back of the resume.)

The important consideration for you is that both of my former employers produced products similar to your company's. In addition, according to your annual report, the corporate structure of all three companies is similar. These similarities mean that you will spend less time training me to fill the position at your company. Hopefully, these qualifications will allow you to consider my application in preference to others who applied.

Sincerely,

John Paul Mueller

6-4
Example cover letter.

certification to increase your chances of getting a job. Make sure you tailor your resume to meet the needs of your future employer.

- Always stress the importance of a particular qualification using placement, type style, and persuasive text. For example, you might want to use bold type to emphasize your Novell certification in the education section of your resume. You might want to stress the importance of the certification in the experience section.
- Never make your resume over two pages long. A one- or two-page resume is what most employers are looking for. If you have more experience and education than you can fit on two pages, then you will

need to tailor it so everything fits. Tell the employer about the qualifications that make you a good candidate for the job. You can talk about other qualifications during the interview or after you get hired.

- Use short clear sentences to express your thoughts. Avoid using complex words in the resume. Don't bury your future employer in archaic and unnecessarily long sentences that don't express your ideas any better than a short one would. If you do need to use some jargon within the resume to fully express your qualifications, try to add some explanatory text as well.
- Structure is the key element in a good resume. Make sure your future employer can find the information he or she is looking for quickly and easily. Use the same strategy of headings and subheadings that a book publisher would use to segment various parts of your resume.
- Include only the information that is relevant to the job. No employer that is looking for a network administrator cares that you pumped gas in high school or that you worked as a cashier for a department store. The only interest they have is in the skills and experience that will help them. Everything else will take up space and bore the person reading the resume.

As you can see, there are quite a few things you can do to make your resume a tool for the employer to use in deciding to hire you. Don't hurt your chances of getting a job by creating a poorly designed resume. Take the time to write something that you and your future employer can discuss during the interview. Always double emphasize the qualifications that the employer is looking for when possible. For example, when you tell your future employer about your Novell certification, include it in both the education and experience sections of your resume.

Now that you have some ideas about what to include in your resume and how to present it to an employer, it's time to look at an example. Figure 6-5 is an example of an experience-based resume. Figure 6-6 is an example of an education-based resume. Notice that each resume provides a different view of the information. This flexibility helps you tailor your resume to the employer's needs.

The first resume uses a lot of white space and bold lettering to draw the reader's attention to particular areas of the document. This helps the manager read the highlights of your resume quickly, then concentrate on any important areas. The resume is slightly over one page, but all the information relates to the position offered by the company. The author mentions network experience twice in the experience section and once in the education section. There is a special computer languages section that draws the manager's attention to the special qualifications of this candidate. Notice that this special qualification is mentioned in the experience and education areas as well. The resume writer does a good job of relating the special qualification back to networking in the first paragraph of the resume. (Knowing computer languages is a good asset for network administrators who need to administer large database management systems.) The writer also spells out each acronym the first time it appears in the document. This is an important part of writing a resume.

The second resume looks somewhat the same as the first one. It uses the same amount of white space and the same bold lettering. However, this resume places education first. Notice that the certifications appear as an entire category by themselves. This tells the reader that your certifications are something of great value that you have to offer. The rest of the educational skills appear second to the all-important job skills. Notice that the job information in this case is very short and concise. The emphasis here is on education supported by experience, not the other way around.

Everyone knows the basics of going in for an interview. You're supposed to get dressed up and present a clean appearance. Of course, breath mints and a good attitude are important too. All these things are just a part of any interview. However, there are several things you can do to enhance your interview by leveraging your Novell certification. The following paragraphs provide you with some ideas on how to do this.

Emphasizing your qualifications during an interview

- Many Novell certificate holders receive lapel pins. Make sure you wear this pin on your lapel during the interview. It serves to reinforce your qualifications every time your potential employer looks at you and sees it.
- Take your ID card along with you. Your employer might ask you to present proof of your certification.
- Prepare a list of the hardware you have worked on in the past. You can use this information during the interview.
- Create a list of questions you want to ask the employer. Every employer asks if you have any questions. Make sure your questions are based on your knowledge of the company and what it does. This is your opportunity to impress the employer with your knowledge of their company.
- The interview is a two-way street, they are not only interviewing you but you are interviewing the company as well. You need to make sure that this is the company you want to invest your time and effort into. Just because you conducted some preliminary research on the company doesn't mean they are a good company to work for. The only time you find this information out is during your conversation with your prospective boss. The company must also pass your interview of them.
- During the interview make sure that you maintain eye contact with the person giving the interview and speak clearly and portray confidence in

yourself. If asked a question that you do not know the answer to, do not make one up. It's better to say that you don't know the answer than to lie to them; it shows honesty. You can usually avoid looking like a dunce when this happens by showing interest in the topic. Use the occasion to feed your potential boss' ego. Phrases like, "I didn't know that" go a long way toward making the interview a success. Make sure you show an interest in what the boss knows and what the company needs rather than irritation at not knowing the answer to a question.

John Mueller
2020 Twin Palms Street
River City, Ca.   92104
Home Phone: 619-775-2123

EXPERIENCE:

Network Administrator, Technical Stuff, Inc. (July 1990–August 1993)

In charge of two assistants at Technical Stuff, Inc. The combination ethernet and Token Ring LAN (local area network) supports 150 users and 4 file servers. There are eight print servers attached to the network as well. Most of the print servers had two printers attached; one HP Laserjet III and a high-speed dot matrix. All maintenance scheduling went through my office. In addition, I supervised the installation of a new DBMS (database management system) on one of the file servers.

6-5
Example experience-based resume.

Assistant Network Administrator, Jobber Industrial (January 1988–July 1990)

Assisted the LAN Administrator in maintaining the company LAN. The LAN supports 40 users and 3 file servers. There are four print servers attached to the network as well. Part of my LAN responsibilities included installing and maintaining Windows. I also performed much of the hardware maintenance.

Sonar Technician, U.S. Navy (July 1976–September 1987)

Maintained computer controlled sonar and fire control equipment. This equipment ranged from tube-based technology to solid-state discrete circuitry to modern CMOS circuitry. Learned to operate and maintain every type of data storage device available today. Most equipment was hybrid digital and analog circuitry.

Designed and was paid for a design change to audio recording equipment. Change decreased recording reproduction time by a factor of four, reducing the per-recording cost to the government for a training tape.

Operated sonar equipment that included acoustic signal analysis equipment. Supervised work center personnel. Wrote six-part training course using tapes and training books.

EDUCATION:

Technical Diploma in Electrical Trade, Milwaukee Technical High School, June 1976

Various military electronic equipment maintenance courses:
- Basic Electronics and Electricity
- Sonar Specific Advanced Electronics
- Acoustic Analysis Schooling
- Fire Control System Maintenance/Operation Schooling
- Computer Controlled Sonar Maintenance/Operation Schooling
- Other Peripheral Equipment Maintenance Schooling

Bachelors in Computer Science, National University, June 1986

Artificial Intelligence Programming course, Cubic Corporation, October 1986

Certified Netware Engineer courses, VITEK Corporation, April 1991

COMPUTER LANGUAGES:

- Pascal—IBM PC knowledge only
- BASIC—IBM PC and Perkin-Elmer mainframe experience (includes various Windows 3.1 dialects such as Access BASIC and Visual BASIC)
- Assembler—IBM PC (DOS, OS/2, and Windows NT environments), Macintosh, and various military computers
- dBase III (Clipper, Force, and FoxPro)—IBM PC
- Prolog—Learning stages, IBM PC knowledge only
- Machine Code (Hex)—IBM PC, Macintosh, and various military computers
- C—IBM PC (DOS, OS/2, and Windows NT environments)

NOVELL.

Robert Williams
9845 Harbor Road Suite 22
Some Region, CA 92112
619-234-7890

CERTIFICATIONS:

1991   LanAlyzer Basic and Advanced for Ethernet
Network Technologies
Novell 3.11 Advanced System Manager

1990   Novell Certified Instructor (CNI) Category I and II
Novell certified to teach:
286 System Manager
Update and Advanced Features
386 OS/Features Review
386 System Supervisor
Service and Support
Novell Enhanced Support Training
Introduction to Data Communications

1989   Novell Certified Engineer (CNE)

EDUCATION:

6-6
Example education-based resume.

1989   Novell Authorized Education.
System Manager
Update and Advanced Features
Service and Support
Diagnostics and Troubleshooting
Introduction to Data Communications
Novell Enhanced Support Training
Novell 386 Training

1987   St. San Antonio College, Walnut, CA
Construction Estimating
Elements of Construction
4.0 G.P.A.

1977   Citrus College, Azusa, CA
Industrial Engineering Technology
3.8 G.P.A.

EXPERIENCE:

Very Impressive Systems, Hard Rock, CA (1989–Present)

Novell Authorized Distributor, Novell Authorized Education Center, Distribution center for major brands of computer equipment.

Novell Certified Instructor: Duties include education of resellers and end users in the use of the Novell Operating System. The classes include 286 System Manager, Update and Advanced Features, 386 OS/Features Review, 386 System Supervisor, Service and Support,

Introduction to Data Communications, Novell Enhanced Support Training, Basic and Intermediate DOS, and Hardware Basics.

Other duties include operating and maintaining the Education Facility in San Diego, CA

Great West Computers, Hard Rock, CA (1989–1989)

Novell Authorized Reseller, Novell Authorized Education Center, Network Installations, Technical Support.

Service and Support Technician: Duties include technical support for customers, education of customers on the use of the Novell operating system, network sales.

Conclusion

This chapter discussed three essential pieces of information you need to use your certification to your advantage. First, we examined the ways you can use your certification to advance within your current company. This is an important consideration if you are happy with your current place of employment. It pays to work with management whenever possible to improve your current employment situation based on new knowledge or experience you gain. Making management aware of all the ways that this new certification can help the company is one way to ensure you continue to advance at a rate that meets your needs.

The second and third sections of this chapter addressed the needs of the person who wants to start fresh after they get their certification. Perhaps management at your company is unable or unwilling to recognize your new level of knowledge. You might simply want to work in a different area of town or move to a new city. Whatever your reason for leaving one company and looking for a new one, you need to address two issues: writing a cover letter and resume and going for an interview. The second section of this chapter addressed the need to improve your resume. Think of your resume as the sales brochure that's going to get you a better job. If you receive as much junk mail as most people, you know that it's the good brochures that attract your attention. The situation is no different for a prospective employer; they get a lot of resumes in the mail. It is your job to make sure you sell them on your qualifications with your resume.

Finally, if you do a good job of selling the prospective employer with your resume, you'll get called in for a job interview. Surprisingly, it's not the slick person in the formal suit or dress that makes the best impression, it's the person who can sell their qualifications. The salesperson gets the job. (Of course, appearance does play an important role in convincing someone to hire you.)

Reading this chapter should help you prepare for career enhancement based on your skills. This is not a movie; don't let the underdog steal a position specially designed for you. Take the time to prepare.

7 Planning for continuing education requirements

You have finally made it! The certification level that you so diligently worked for is finally yours! Take some time to feel good about yourself and your accomplishments. After all, you have worked hard for it and you deserve it. Once you have had time to reflect on your accomplishments, you must begin to think about and plan for what it will take to maintain your precious certification. The certification that you have obtained, while yours at the moment, is revocable by Novell if you do not meet the continuing education requirements.

Introduction

These requirements are not difficult and are not an every-other-month demand to squeeze more money out of you. Novell only asks you to recertify if there is a major change in networking technology. These requirements are a necessary request by Novell to keep your knowledge of the products current. You are Novell's best representative and salesperson because you are the one that is on the frontline with the customer. If your knowledge of the product is not current or not accurate, Novell's credibility as well as yours will come into question. The last thing you want is to have a customer think that Novell or your skills are not what they expected. If this customer is not comfortable with Novell's reputation or yours, they will probably take their business elsewhere. What this means to you is that you lose a potential sale of your services resulting in a loss of income to you and Novell.

The process of planning for continuing education does not stop at what Novell requires of you. This only skims the surface of what you need to know in the real world to conduct business. You must enhance your scope of knowledge to keep an edge in this industry. This chapter discusses what your continuing education responsibilities are in maintaining your Novell certification. Because the education process does not stop with Novell training, we will also cover topics that help you remain current in the networking market. These additional topics include where to find valuable information about networking. The ideas in this chapter are certainly only a beginning. As you gain experience and accumulate time in the networking business, you will find your own additional sources of continuing education that will meet your particular needs.

Looking for more information

The real expert in this business, be it the system administrator, consultant, analyst, instructor, or anyone else, has a desire for more information. It's like an obsession. The more information and knowledge that you have, the more you want. This is probably the only industry where the more you learn about a topic the more you find that you know so little. It is also the only industry where technology changes and advances so fast that the trade journals have a hard time keeping up.

The key to staying current is finding the information that pertains to your situation. We are living in an age of information. The problem that faces most of us is information overload. The faster you read the information, the faster it seems to arrive. Every vendor wants you to know about their great new product. Every magazine says that they are the key resource you need to improve your business. The way to control information overload is to know what and where your interests lie. Many times a consultant tries to use the shotgun approach when trying to absorb this vast array of information. He or she tries to look at everything and remember each piece or detail of information. This is usually not the best way.

To help you remember more of the facts and information pieces, focus on the topics that interest you. Do not spend time on topics that are of little interest to you. For example suppose that you are a system administrator of a small firm with 10 to 12 users, you are using Novell NetWare v2.2 with no access or connections to a mainframe computer. Unless you are personally interested in mainframe computers and might someday need this information, allocate your time to gathering information about products and techniques related to local area networks (LANs). This is not to say that all the other information sent your way is not important or worthwhile, because it is. You need to remember where your priorities lie and what your main interests are. Make a mental note of this other information for future reference. If you need this information someday, you will know where to start looking for it. Figure 7-1 helps you get a handle on what information you need to read. It contains a survey of the things you need to read about to maintain your client's or company's LAN in the peak of condition.

Name: _____ Date: _____

Position: _____

Hardware Needs:

❑ PC

❑ Macintosh

❑ Mainframe

❑ Minicomputer

Software Needs:

Word Processing: _____ Database: _____

Spreadsheet: _____ Accounting: _____

Communications: _____ Other: _____

Peripheral devices:

❑ Tape Drive

❑ Sound Board

❑ MODEM

❑ Printers: _____

❑ Other: _____

❑ CD-ROM/WORM Drive

❑ Mouse

_____

_____

Network Specific:

Network type: _____ Bridges/Routers: _____

Operating system version: _____ Print servers: _____

Other: _____ _____

7-1
Reading interest survey.

The survey provides you with some ideas of what you need to read to maintain your network. Simply fill out the form and then look for those areas in the magazines and trade papers that you need to read. There is another way that you can use this survey. Some people get so much mail and so many magazines to read that even a focused approach to reading will not help them get through everything they need to look at. They usually resort to using a clipping service (a company that sends you clippings from magazines and trade papers in your areas of interest). A more cost-effective method of doing the same thing is to have a secretary or other assistant use the survey as a means for going through magazines and trade papers for you. They simply clip out the articles that you are interested in. This alleviates the need to go through all the magazines and trade papers. It also helps you maintain your concentration level by removing sources of nonessential information.

The basic information needed to maintain your certification will come from Novell in some fashion. This might include instructor-led courses, videotapes, manuals, bulletins, or seminars. This information is very Novell specific and relates only to Novell, NetWare products, and your certification. Because most people have an interest in the complete scope of networking, using Novell as your only source of information will not get you very far. For this reason other sources of information include magazines, trade papers, books, on-line services, and electronic media.

These other sources of information will help you to maintain your Novell certification, and will help you to advance to the next level of certification or a better job. Do not fall into the trap many people do by thinking that now that I have my certification I can stop studying. Nothing could be further from the truth. Now that you have your certification you must work just as hard to maintain it.

As you wade through the reams of paper and screens of electronic information, you need to develop a method or style for processing this information. There is so much information available that it's not practical for you to try to memorize all of it. It is even harder to find where you saw the information if you can only remember some small part of what you read.

One way that helps you organize this information in a retrievable fashion is to photocopy the table of contents. Put the photocopied table of contents in a notebook. Divide the notebook into sections such as magazines, trade papers, books, electronic sources, and others. You can also divide it by magazine/trade paper title. Ordering your magazine and trade paper articles in this manner allows you to quickly locate what you need. Of course, part of this maintenance includes removing old information from the folder. For example, you wouldn't want to keep articles that told you about the latest version of the PC—the 8088. Keeping your information up to date is part of the work required to reduce information overload.

Another way to reference information is to use a program such as AskSam or Folio Views. Folio Views is the same program Novell uses for their on-line help and the NetWare Buyer's Guide (the NetWare Buyer's Guide is discussed later in this chapter). With this program you can quickly and easily create an infobase with all the previously mentioned information. You can also add a paraphrased summary of the articles, books, or other information to help narrow your search of a particular topic. In fact, you can scan entire articles into the database using a scanner. While this requires a little more time creating and maintaining the infobase, you will be able to find the information that you are looking for faster. Other methods of recalling this information may include creating a database using one of the popular database programs or converting the data into an electronic format that's retrievable at a later time using a computer. Whatever methods you use to keep track of the important information you find, the key is to record and document your findings. Do not entrust this information to memory.

Ziff Publishing provides a unique method for accessing their articles and reviews. You can order *Computer Library Plus* for a nominal fee. Every month you receive a new CD-ROM disk containing the latest articles and reviews about any topic you can think of. The CD contains the complete text (excluding graphics and advertisements) of over 170 publications. It also includes 13,000 company profiles and a complete computer glossary. The search engine included as part of the library system allows you to conduct keyword searches throughout the entire database. You can order *Computer Library Plus* by calling 1-800-827-7889. The cost is about $1,000 per subscription. Microsoft provides the same type of library through the Microsoft Developer Network. It contains the latest issues of *Microsoft Systems Journal* and many of the Cobb Group newsletters. You can order the Microsoft Developer Network by calling 1-800-227-4679. The cost is about $195 per subscription.

Magazines

Magazines are an excellent source of information. By subscribing to a few good magazines you will be able to remain current on most areas of networking. Many publishers produce their magazines on a biweekly or a monthly basis. Because you have a couple of weeks to read the magazine, you will be able to study when you have the time. You are also better able to absorb and retain what you read if you're not under pressure or rushed.

Finding magazines doesn't present a problem either. There are many excellent magazines on the shelves at your favorite bookstore. You will also find that there are as many magazines that never make it to the bookstores or magazine racks. It's not that these magazines are of any less quality, they just have a different market targeted. They usually get mailed directly to your home or business. You can usually find business reply cards for these magazines in the card stacks you get in the mail, as part of software packages, or within other magazines. For example, most of the Cobb Group newsletters are sold as part of the software packages you purchase. They also have direct mail based on the registration cards you send back to the vendor.

Deciding which ones you will buy is a very difficult decision and one you should not rush. Spend time researching each one of them, looking for the ones that center on the topics that concern you. You can't buy and read every one of them. Even if you had the money to do so, it would require many hours or days to read them all. You must narrow your choice to the few good magazines that address your areas of interest. By reading the magazines written with a focus on your area of interest, you won't have to wade through articles you have no interest in.

Many magazines on the newsstands contain too many advertisements, and in some cases, ads get top priority over the articles. This becomes very annoying when the articles seem too short or the editor leaves out important information because the ads needed more room. Sometimes you can't get around these types of magazines. Even though they have a lot of ads, they still contain some good information. As you spend time looking at magazines month after month you will begin to notice which ones are ads magazines and which ones have the substance of good articles.

You will also begin to see patterns in the types of articles written for the different magazines. Some magazines are into home computing, some the latest gadgets, others focus on networking, and still others cover every other aspect of computers or electronics. Find the ones that deal with your needs. These magazines should become part of your required reading list. Make sure that you read them each month; they are your windows into the industry. Always read the articles that are of importance to you first. Then spend some time skimming the other articles to get an overview of what they are trying to convey. If you find something interesting, then read it. After you have read the required magazines, then read any others if you have time or want to. If you try to read everything you are just wasting your time.

For the Novell expert there are two magazines that you should not miss: *LAN Times* and *NetWare Application Notes*. McGraw-Hill publishes *LAN Times* which is basically a Novell-based magazine. This biweekly publication covers everything taking place within the PC networking industry. Although it is a Novell-based magazine, it is also one of the most objective magazines available. The magazine includes articles on the latest technologies, internetworking, applications, and network management to name a few. There is also an article in every issue that covers a "hands-on" topic. This article covers some networking-specific topic, usually directly relating in some way to Novell, giving you theory, use, and procedures.

The second magazine that is a must-read publication is *NetWare Application Notes*. This is a Novell published magazine that goes into great depth on the topic being covered. There are usually three to five articles in each publication with absolutely no ads. The articles cover such topics as installation, integration, testing, theory, and management to name a few. When you become a CNE, Novell sends you one complementary copy of the *Application Notes*, also referred to as "APP Notes." If you want to continue to receive the magazine after that, and we recommend that you do, you can find the ordering information inside the front cover of the magazine.

Many other magazines also deal with PC networks. You need to research each of them to find the ones appropriate for you and your needs. Some of the magazines are free to consultants, administrators, and businesses. When you find a magazine you like, call or write to the circulation manager and ask about a complimentary subscription. Many times you will find that complimentary subscriptions are available for the asking. Sometimes they are on a trial offer of one to three issues for free. If you cannot get them for free then spend the money for them; you need some access to the technology. In most cases, magazine subscriptions are tax deductible as a business expense or education expense.

Once you finish reading a magazine, remember to document the contents and store the publication in a safe place. You will only remember a small fraction of the information contained within the articles, but by using some form of documentation you will be able to access the information when you need it in the future.

As your experience and knowledge change so should the magazines, trade papers, and books you buy. If you find that a particular publication is no longer teaching or informing you, then it might be time to drop the subscription. If you keep reading the same material that you already know then you are just wasting your time.

Trade papers

The weekly trade papers that you receive are packed with the latest information about the computer industry. Subscriptions to a few of the more popular ones will keep you up to date on what the hardware and software vendors are doing. They always have articles about new gadgets, state-of-the-art technology, and trends. Also included are columns about what certain industry people are doing and what company they are working for this week.

As with magazines, you must find the ones that meet your needs and make them your top reading priority. There are just too many on the market to read every one of them. Some of the papers you will find are very pro IBM or UNIX, while others only concern themselves with what Novell is doing, or what Microsoft is doing. Whenever you see articles of this type in a magazine or trade paper, remember that they only express the opinion of the author. These articles do not necessarily represent the right or wrong view of the industry, simply one person's view. Of course, these people maintain their position because they are either controversial or correct more often than not. Whichever papers you decide to get, make sure that they objectively cover the topics that interest you.

The trade papers, when read in addition to regular subscriptions of books and magazines, will keep you informed about the industry. You will find that trade papers have a lot of articles that are unrelated to what you are doing and contain a ton of ads. Like magazines, publishers send trade papers directly to your home or place of business on a weekly or regular basis.

When reading the trade papers, keep in mind some of the same ideas for documenting the contents of each one as practiced with the magazines. Find the articles of interest, make photocopies of them, then place the articles in a binder. Record the entries in a table of contents for future reference. After you save the articles that interest you, discard the original trade paper or recycle it. If you try to save every back issue, you will soon find that you need a large storage garage to keep them all.

A few of the trade papers that you might want to invest in are *Network World, Computer Technology Review, Computer Reseller News, PC Week*, and *LAN Times*. By taking some or all of these, you will have complete coverage of the industry. If you wish to order these trade papers or contact them, the phone numbers and addresses are in appendix B.

Books The use of books is another excellent source of information for continuing education. There are books written on most subjects and they can be very useful for later reference. You will find that in a very short time you will have a complete library. Plan for this growth by investing in a good bookcase with plenty of room. It might have a couple of empty shelves now, but it won't take long to fill them. You will find that by having your books in one place, you are much more apt to refer to the material.

Most of the books written about a software product contain the same information that's supplied by the vendor manuals. The difference between the third-party books and the vendor manuals is that the information written in the third-party books is more concise and useful than the manuals. They often have real-world examples written in terms that most readers can easily understand. While these books contain a large amount of information, they are not for everyone. Most of the material will not be of interest to you if you have much experience with a product. It will be more of a review for you than an education. However, the books can serve as reference material and you will get another point of view on a subject.

For the dedicated NetWare professional, one book that should be mandatory for your library is the *NetWare Buyer's Guide.* This is a Novell published book that is usually updated twice a year. This book is free of charge by calling Novell. The *NetWare Buyer's Guide* is available in both a paper version and an electronic version. The electronic version has the same appearance and interface as the Novell help utility with NetWare. Novell divides the contents of the *NetWare Buyer's Guide* into four sections:

1. Novell Corporate and Strategic Overview—This section details Novell's company background, market leadership, and Novell integrated computing architecture. The role that Novell plays in computer networking is defined, as well as the concepts of Novell networks operating with other computer vendors. Also included in this section is the theory of operations for the Novell operating systems.
2. Novell Product Overview—Section two outlines all the products Novell sells and supports in an overview fashion. Described in this section is the history of the Novell products and the reasons for using them. Because this section is an overview of Novell products, there is no discussion of the actual workings of the products. All CNAs, CNEs, ECNEs, CNIs, administrators, consultants, and anyone that is working with the Novell operating system should read this section. You will learn about all the different products that Novell has to offer. Many times knowing what products are available can give you ideas about making your system work better.
3. Novell Products—Listed in this chapter are the Novell products. This section lists products by type: operating system, network services, communication services, internetwork, network connectivity, network management, and distributed application development tools. Under each heading is a listing of every Novell product that relates to that topic. The products are in an overview fashion, this time with more technical information. This section also explains the features of the products and what makes them useful to you and why you need them. Other information includes implementation, required hardware and software, along with any other options required to complete the job. The final part of this section covers specifications and ordering information, along with part numbers. This is an

excellent section for learning how each product works and what the hardware and software requirements are.

4. Novell Support and Education—This section deals with the customer support programs offered by Novell for both resellers and end users. The information in this section is an overview of Novell services including technical support, NetWire information, and the reseller authorization program. Also included is an overview of the Novell education and training programs.

The *NetWare Buyer's Guide* is an asset to your reference library and will prove useful to you in learning about Novell products. Whether you work with the book version or the electronic version, be sure to contact Novell on a regular basis for an upgrade to your *NetWare Buyer's Guide*.

On-line services   Novell offers a wide range of services to all NetWare users and support technicians. Besides the standard publications of magazines and books, Novell offers electronic on-line services as well. With these services you can use your computer to stay in touch with Novell.

The on-line Novell services fall into two categories: dial-in voice services and computer access services. The dial-in voice service includes Novell's technical information service, update information service, education information and enrollment, and direct product ordering service. This service is available seven days a week and 24 hours a day. If you have technical questions about any Novell products and would like to talk to a Novell technician, you can call the Novell technical support department. As a CNE, Novell provides you two free incident calls the first year of your certification. If after two calls or the first year of certification you need more technical support, you can purchase additional support for a reduced rate.

Other services that you can take advantage of include ordering of Novell products including updates to current products. You can also obtain information about the NAECs and listings of the latest courses.

NetWire   For the latest up-to-date information about Novell or NetWare products, Novell offers the services of NetWire. This is a type of bulletin board service. The NetWire service, referred to as the Novell forum or NetWire forum, is available through CompuServe. Once you have access to CompuServe, the NetWire services are then free.

Sysops (system operators) perform the maintenance and control of the NetWire forum. In the case of NetWire, the sysops are Novell employees and volunteer Novell experts. These men and women monitor the files being uploaded and downloaded on the system. They are also available to answer any questions that you might have about where to find information, how to use the forums, and to answer any technical questions you might have concerning Novell and their products.

One of the services offered by NetWire is the posting of questions about NetWare onto the forum. Anyone having access to the forum can read and answer these questions. The answers to the questions you post on the forum can come from the other users or the sysops. These users are people that might be end users, system administrators, CNEs, CNIs, or anyone else with an interest in Novell. With thousands of people using NetWire every day, and many of them reading the questions, there is a very good chance that someone will be able to answer your questions.

Other services offered by the NetWire service are product updates and conferences. Product updates include the latest patches, fixes, drivers, and enhancements available for the Novell product line. These updates are downloadable from the service and are free to users of NetWire. The other service—conferences—allows a group of NetWire users to have an on-line discussion about some topic. Some of these discussions are preplanned and conducted by a Novell sysop or engineer, or they can be a spur of the moment conference with a group of users. The topics range from a problem someone has been having to the theory and implementation of some technology.

NetWire forums and services make it a source of information for CNAs, CNEs, ECNEs, or CNIs. You will find that the cost of the CompuServe service is at times more justifiable than using the Novell technical support. It is also a definite asset for obtaining the most current drivers and patches. For more information about CompuServe and NetWire refer to appendix B.

FaxBack   The Novell FaxBack service, as mentioned in chapter 3 is another electronic service offered by Novell. This service is part of the Novell education department and allows you to receive by fax a listing of the authorized education centers and class information. Besides the list of NAECs and course information, you can get general information about CNA, CNE, ECNE, and CNI certifications. Also available is training information about the Univel product, general Novell education information, Novell education area managers, and self-study products sold by Novell. The FaxBack service offered by Novell is a good way to find information about certifications and education without having to contact the CNA/CNE/ECNE division every time you have a question.

Novell offers a product called the Network Support Encyclopedia (NSE). This is an electronic information base containing technical data about

Electronic media

Novell networking. The NSE comes in two versions: the standard volume and the professional volume. The standard volume contains Novell's technical notes, hardware and software test information, product documentation and product information, product specifications, NetWire information, Novell press releases, and the *NetWare Buyer's Guide*.

The NSE professional version includes all the information included in the standard version along with downloadable information. The downloadable information is the same information that is available on NetWire. Some of the things that are downloadable include NetWare patches, product fixes, device drivers, product enhancements, troubleshooting charts, the *NetWare Application Notes*, and additional manuals. The NSE standard volume is available in both a diskette version and a CD-ROM version, while the NSE professional volume is only available on CD-ROM. Novell updates both versions on a regular basis: the diskette version once a quarter and the CD-ROM version once a month.

Once you become a CNE, you will receive one issue of the NSE professional version in either the diskette version or the CD-ROM version. If you want to receive updates for your NSE, you have to contact Novell and buy them. While these updates are not mandatory, they are well worth the investment.

CNE continuing education requirements

You must update your certification from time to time as a CNE. These continuing education requirements are to help you maintain a certain level of expertise with Novell products. This also helps Novell in marketing a product because the customer can receive qualified support. The continuing education requirements are usually only necessary when Novell introduces a new product, and then only if they feel that all CNEs should be aware of the updates. The required updates to your certification are usually only once every one or two years. If there is a certification update Novell will notify you by mail of the necessary requirements. After Novell notifies you of the update, you have 90 days to fulfill the requirements, which normally requires passing the competency exam. If you do not know the new material, Novell and NAECs offer classes. Even though you have 90 days to meet the certification requirements, don't wait too long. Try to recertify as soon as possible, but make sure you give yourself plenty of time to prepare for the exam. Remember that the more pressure you are under, the higher the odds are of failing.

ECNE continuing education requirements

Continuing education requirements are also applicable for the ECNE. Any of the certification updates required for the CNE are also a requirement to maintain your ECNE certification (since you must be a CNE before you can become an ECNE). There might also be recertification requirements that apply only to ECNEs. If Novell feels that a product or technology is important and ECNEs should know about it, they will add it to the continuing education requirement list. Because the ECNE is a more specialized person, Novell makes sure that they have knowledge of these new products.

The Novell CNI is a little different from the CNE and ECNE when it comes to recertification. The Novell certification for the CNI allows them to teach either category I, category II, or specialized classes. If Novell releases a new product and has an instructor-led class that covers the material, then the CNI has to update their certification in order to teach that class. If, for example, a new operating system has a system administration course offered, chances are that class will fall in the category I set of classes. If an instructor wants to maintain their category I certification then they must complete any of the new certification requirements. The new certification usually involves attending the course. These classes are taught either by a Novell-employed instructor or at an NAEC by an already certified instructor. After completing the course and receiving the certificate, the instructor must pass the CNI version of the proficiency exam. After passing the exam, the CNI must fax a copy of the course certificate to the CNI administration department. When the CNI candidate satisfies these requirements, Novell permits the CNI to teach the course.

Another requirement is that the CNI must attend an instructor evaluation class (IEC) to remain certified. In the IEC the instructor conducts lectures on the material that will be part of the course. The instructor must pass a critique that's based on presentation skills and technical accuracy. Most of the time the instructor has to attend only the IEC if they wish to teach the ECNE or specialty classes. Another possible requirement for CNIs is to attend a seminar-style class. At this seminar a Novell-employed instructor presents information that Novell considers essential for the CNIs to know. The CNI might or might not have an exam on this material.

The instructor must be sure to stay up to date on all continuing education requirements because they are the ones at the front of the classroom trying to teach the material. If the instructor does not fully comprehend the material it cannot be fully explained to the students.

Conclusion

The need for more information is an ongoing quest for the person with interest in maintaining a network. The requirements and level of knowledge might be different between the CNA and the CNI, but the need is still there. The information you seek might be for general interest or to satisfy a need to maintain your Novell certification. In either case, using magazines, trade papers, and books will help you become more efficient at what you are doing. Just because you obtain your Novell certification doesn't mean you can stop learning. You must now prepare yourself for recertification requirements.

As you find information in magazines, trade papers, books, and other sources, remember to organize your material in a way that will be retrievable in the future. As you acquire stacks of publications in your library, you will find that the time spent researching back information will become tremendous if it is not properly documented. By using the ideas presented in this chapter, such as photocopying the table of contents from the publications and storing them in a binder, you will be able to narrow your search for information.

The continuing education requirements are an important part of maintaining a level of competency for a Novell certification. The higher the level of customer satisfaction, the better the chances are that Novell will maintain dominance in the market. This will create a better market for Novell-certified people, as well as more jobs and higher incomes. Both the CNE and the ECNE continuing education requirements might seem like a waste of time, effort, and money, but they are a necessity to maintain the proper level of expertise. Without the extra requirements, there would be many CNEs with an incomplete understanding of Novell and the products they sell and support. When recertifying, remember that you are enhancing your marketability in the networking industry.

8 The consulting approach

Many consultants make a living installing and maintaining Novell local area networks (LANs). Installing and maintaining LANs became a very lucrative business when large corporations decided to downsize their database applications from mainframes and minicomputers to PCs. In addition, many small businesses are starting to see the benefits of networking their computers to enhance productivity. Add to this the increasing number of middle-size businesses and you have a climate ripe for the entrepreneur. As the business market gets more competitive, the consultant should see an increase in business.

Introduction

Of course, not every consultant will see an increase in their customer base. The difference between a successful consultant and one that simply maintains their current installed base is recognition. Unless you get recognition for your achievements as a businessperson, there is little chance that you will increase your client base.

There are other benefits to enhancing your knowledge level than simply working more hours per day as your client base increases in size. For example, with an increase in capability you can charge higher per-hour fees. You might find that you can afford to hire a helper. This allows you to concentrate on the "fun" jobs and give someone else the headaches. As you can see, the benefits to a Novell certification are many. However, to get the benefits you must first gain recognition.

This chapter specifically targets the networking expert. It provides the consultant with ideas on how to improve their business through proper use of Novell supplied aids. It also examines some of the ways that the consultant can use a certification to gain and keep new clients. Finally, this chapter examines some thorny issues like what to charge the client for network services and how to maintain a professional relationship with the client.

Using the Novell logo

Once you get your certification you need to tell people about it. Clients usually aren't thrilled about wasting time hearing about your latest achievement, so you need to tell them in an almost subliminal manner. One of the ways you can do this is to add the Novell logo to all your business correspondence, price lists, business cards, and other advertisements. The following paragraphs discuss some of the ways you can use the Novell logo to tell your clients about your capabilities.

Advertisements

There are two elements to advertising: design and distribution. The first topic is subject to much debate. The number and variety of advertising brochures you get in the mail demonstrates this. The second topic is a little easier for the consultant to master. As a consultant, there are only a handful of truly effective ways to distribute your advertisements.

Let's tackle the first problem: how to design your brochure. Your best source of information on how to solve this problem is the junk mail you receive. What kinds of mail attract your attention? Give the same junk mail to a few people willing to help you out. Ask them to show you which junk mail attracts their attention. Now, throw the rest of the junk mail away (unless you really need it). Going through all the mail that attracts your attention will give you ideas about what works and what doesn't. You might want to perform the same kind of analysis on magazine advertisements and store brochures if you intend to pursue those routes. Always look at what the successful competition is doing, then add a few ideas of your own to come up with a truly winning combination.

Once you get a few ideas together you need to create an advertisement. Creating an advertising brochure is not a scientific process; it lies on the artistic edge of maintaining a business. Of course, part of the problem is that an effective advertising brochure usually attracts our attention because we can understand what the author is trying to say. As a result, a brochure that works fine in one area of the country might fail in another part because the cultural connection isn't as strong. When someone calls your business, you might want to take the time to ask them why they called. Keep track of what types of advertising work and what types don't. Make sure you weigh the scores to account for the types of client you like to work with. If your advertising always attracts the wrong kind of client, it's a sure sign that you need to create a different type of brochure.

There are several common elements that you need to put in a brochure. First, you need to identify yourself. Unless people know who they're dealing with, you won't get any sales. Second, you need to consider adding a list of services. You can do this in a number of ways. For example, stores usually use graphics to tell people what services they offer. (What else do you call a picture of a computer with a price listed below it?) Some businesses use a simple list that looks much like a price list. Still other businesses use descriptive paragraphs or other methods to tell people what services they offer. The choice is up to you. You might want to include prices as part of your brochure, but this usually isn't the best idea for consultants. Keeping your price as part of a price list that you give the client after you make your sales pitch is usually a better idea. Of course, every form of advertising you create should contain your Novell certification. Have you ever noticed how other vendors use this technique to attract potential clients? You need to avail yourself of this potential sales tool as well. Make sure you look at these other sales brochures for ideas on how to present your certification. You should consider including the actual logo as part of your advertisement and adding some text that says, "Fully Novell certified to work on your network."

The second problem that you need to deal with is distribution. Some businesses resort to mass mailings and all kinds of other methods to attract new clients. While this might work fine for your local food store, it usually doesn't work all that well for a networking professional. Studies show that response to mass mailings is approximately 7 to 10 percent. So how do you get new clients? An advertising brochure is still a good method of gaining new clients, but the method of distribution can make all the difference in the world.

Word of mouth is a very good method for a consultant to gain new clients. Other professionals, such as doctors and lawyers, have relied on this method of gaining new clients for years. Have you ever noticed the other method that these professionals use? Referrals are a common method of gaining new clients in both of these fields. A generalist will refer you to a specialist for a particular kind of work. The same holds true for professionals certified by Novell. You need to rely on both word of mouth and referrals for new clients. However, the job doesn't end there. The computer business is a lot more complex than other businesses. Every day there are new developments in the industry that other people might not know about. Certainly they won't know everything you do about your business. The reason for advertising becomes very clear when you look at it from this perspective.

You might find that your local newspaper or computer magazine is a good place to advertise. This is a secondary means of gaining new clients to word of mouth and referrals. Experience shows that about 50 percent of people respond to either word of mouth or referral. Only 1 percent of the people you reach with a magazine advertisement will respond. Of those who respond, only about 1.5 percent will actually turn into clients. (Results obtained from a survey of 50 computer consultants who relied on all three methods of gaining new clients.) This means that you have to reach a minimum of 10,000 people with your newspaper or magazine advertisement to get a potential client. The numbers for telephone book advertisements are even smaller because the audience is less inclined to need computer services. As you can see, the one or two clients you gain using advertisements need to pay off with large work loads and lots of referrals to make the effort worthwhile.

Brochures, business cards, and price lists

There are three types of documents that do not fall into the advertisement category, but that can act as subtle reminders of the services you offer. They are brochures, business cards, and price lists. All three of these items end up in the hands of your current clients. If you can get the client to look at these items from time to time, the subtle reminders you leave will help them remember what services you offer. They will also serve as reminders to the client to tell others about the services you offer. Remember, referrals are one of the best means at your disposal for gaining new clients.

Business cards offer very little room for advertising, much less subtle reminders. By the time you add a name, address, telephone number, and fax number, there is little room left for anything else. However, you can usually add a logo or two plus a slug line. You normally add your business logo on the same line or directly below the name of your business. The logo identifies your business to people. They might actually look for the logo instead of your name when they look for your business card. Adding your Novell certification logo to the bottom of your business card adds a subtle reminder about one of the services you offer. This little graphic says a lot about you and your business. The slug line usually includes one- or two-word reminders of services you offer or perhaps the guiding ideas of your business. Make sure you add a reference to your Novell certification here as well. It doesn't have to contain many words. Simply saying "Novell Certified" usually gets your point across to the client.

Price lists are a very important part of your business. Some clients might actually believe that you go out of your way to overcharge them if you don't provide such a document. In addition, some clients view the lack of a price list as an indication that you are willing to negotiate on your prices. If you are not willing to make this concession, a price list is the best means of telling the client. Providing them with a document that spells out what you charge and how you apply those charges is very important to maintaining good client relations. You need to make the price list pay some dividend in increased sales or other tangible benefits. This is where adding your Novell certification logo comes into play. Adding something as small and unobtrusive as a logo can provide a big payback. As the client peruses your price list, they also get a complete reminder of why you charge more than Joe or Sally down the street. Your certification logo reminds them that they are paying for a higher quality of service than they might otherwise obtain. It also reminds them to tell their friends about the quality service they receive from you. Even a price list can serve as an advertisement. Make sure you get the full benefit from the investment you make in this document.

The final document is a brochure. This is a relatively undefined piece of information you provide to the client. This includes everything from advertising brochures (covered in the previous section) to documents designed to help the client use your services more efficiently. For example, how often has the client asked you about what your certification really represents? It makes good sense to create a brochure that tells the client about your certification and why it is important. If your business uses more than one level of certification, you can use a brochure to help the client understand what services they can expect from each of your employees. Make sure you create valuable tools of this type to reduce the time you spend answering client questions. Of course, adding the logo to brochures of this type only serves to show the client your level of dedication and professionalism. Make sure you add the certification logo whenever possible.

Carrying your ID card

The first thing that comes to many people's minds about a badge is identification. It is true that your Novell ID card will identify you to your clients. It provides them with a picture, a name, and a certification number they can use for reference. This provides the client with a sense of security; they know who you are and what you represent.

If you spend time going from site to site, you soon realize that clients judge you by your appearance and not your professionalism on the first visit. Your manner in dealing with client questions also makes a big impact. A charming idiot will obtain more clients than a surly genius. (Keeping them is another matter; the surly genius who gets the job done usually wins on this count.)

The most obvious answer to the question of physical appearance versus professionalism appears to lie in good communication skills. You want to tell the client who you are and what you represent. Unfortunately, blurting out all your qualifications might make it appear that you're a boastful oaf more than a professional and thoughtful consultant. So how do you tell the client about all your qualifications without making your sales pitch seem rude? Brochures, price lists, and advertisements all help with the sales pitch. However, there is another method that many consultants fail to consider. We all know the importance of dressing for the job and making sure we present a clean appearance, but this only skims the surface. Use subliminal methods to tell people about you and your business. For example, wearing your Novell badge can go a long way toward starting a client initiated conversation about your qualifications. (They might simply ask why you're wearing the badge.) If you can get the client to ask about your qualifications, they are less apt to think you're boasting about your qualifications and more likely to think that you provide complete and reasonable answers to their questions.

Your badge says a lot more than what you can do. Wearing your badge helps people see that your certification means a lot to you. It also shows your professionalism; that you have the knowledge required to keep their network running or to get it installed. People tend to maintain the first impression that they get from you. It is very difficult for a consultant to overcome a negative first impression. Make sure you make the right first impression by helping people see the professional side of your business.

Determining what services to offer

Determining what services you want to offer is a matter of taking inventory of what skills you have to offer and what skills pay the best. You also need to consider what the clients in your area need the most and what they view as most valuable. This is one of the reasons that you decided to pursue your Novell certification. The first part is fairly easy. Simply create a list of your skills and rank them from 1 to 10. Figure 3-1 provided you with an opportunity to survey your networking skills. Figure 8-1 provides the same opportunity with your skills as a whole. Notice that each section provides additional spaces for you to add specialized skills.

Notice that there are four sections to this survey. The first section asks about your hardware experience. The second and third sections ask about your software and training experience respectively. These are the three major areas of participation for a consultant. Of course, there are other areas as well. For example, the fourth section contains a listing for the lucrative area of technical writing. How does each of these areas relate to your Novell certification? As you gain knowledge and experience with networks, your hardware experience will grow. In addition, companies will call on your networking experience when they try to get their software to work. Passing this knowledge to other people is always a marketable skill. And how many times have you walked into a situation where the client had little or no documentation for their network? The need for technical writers becomes obvious when you look at this need. As you can see, you can enhance each of these skills when you get your Novell certification. Marketing these advanced skills is the sign of good business management.

You can answer the second part of the new services equation in two ways. First, you can simply survey or ask your clients what they need in the way of service. You might want to ask them leading questions that produce more than a yes or no answer. Make sure you look at their business for opportunities. You might find that the client hadn't considered this service item in the past. Don't be surprised if the client turns down some of the ideas you have. They might not see a need to pursue them and any arguments on your part could serve to alienate the client. Figure 8-2 is a simple survey you can ask the client to fill out, or you can use it as a reference document when you ask the questions in person.

Hardware

SKILLS	LEVEL									
	High									Low
	10	9	8	7	6	5	4	3	2	1
Cable installation										
Computer system building										
Computer system installation										
Computer system repair/maintenance										
Routers/bridges/hubs/etc.										
Mini and mainframe connections										
Scientific/specialty installations										
Others:										

8-1
Network consultant's skills survey.

8-1 *Continued.*

Software

SKILLS	LEVEL									
	High									**Low**
	10	9	8	7	6	5	4	3	2	1
Programming										
Installation/upgrades										
Configuration management (the software configuration for each machine)										
License management										
Fault resolution (making the hardware and software work together)										
Others:										

Networking (see Fig. 3-12)

Training

SKILLS	LEVEL									
	High									**Low**
	10	9	8	7	6	5	4	3	2	1
Database										
Spreadsheet										
Word processing										
Graphics software										
Custom software										

8-1 *Continued.*

Training

SKILLS	LEVEL									
	High									Low
	10	9	8	7	6	5	4	3	2	1
Graphics software										
Custom software										
Network maintenance/administration										
Hardware maintenance/repair										
Technical support technician										
Peripheral device support (print server support)										
Others:										

Other

SKILLS	LEVEL									
	High									Low
	10	9	8	7	6	5	4	3	2	1
Technical Writing (network documentation and user manuals)										
Others:										

1. In what ways do you see your need for customized software support growing in the future? How far into the future?

2. What types of new products are you planning to build in the future? How will this affect your network?

3. When do you plan to downsize your current mainframe database to a PC LAN?

4. How can we improve the reliability of your network? What types of hardware and software purchases are you willing to support to make these changes?

8-2
Sample customer survey.

5. Are there tasks that you would like the network to perform but that you can't get it to do?

6. Have you considered any contingency plans if the network fails? If so, have you actually tested them?

7. Which methods do you find most effective for protecting your software investment?

8. Are there any other ways you could use my business help in making yours grow?

The sample survey shows you how to phrase an open-ended question. Notice that we didn't ask the client if they planned to expand the number of products they produced, but what types of new products they were planning. This open-ended question assumes that the client's business is in good shape and that they plan to grow. You really wouldn't want to assume anything else. You also want to explore the outer reaches of networking with your questions. For example, the client was asked about their mainframe database. Many clients do not even think of downsizing their current applications until you ask them about it. Make the client see your visions as their own ideas. Asking questions like the ones shown in FIG. 8-2 will make it appear that the client had the idea, not you. (Putting the client into the driver's seat is the easiest way to ensure they will accept any proposals you make as a result of the survey.)

The second way you can answer the question of what services the client needs is to look in your local newspaper and read the case studies in the magazines and trade papers. These sources of information serve as a source of ideas for questions that you can add to your survey. You might even want to offer the service and see how many clients respond. Often a client will say they are not interested in a service if you ask them first, but respond favorably if the service is already in place.

Your clients might not even know what your certification means. After all, until you read this book you might not have known what certification involved or what you would get out of it. Your clients are probably less informed than you are about Novell certification, yet this is one area that they really do need to know about. It always pays to keep your clients informed. A little information goes a long way when it comes to helping the client see the need for a particular course of action.

As a Novell certified professional you can usually charge a little more than your noncertified competition for the same service. The reason is simple; you have demonstrated that you possess a set of fully developed skills while the competition hasn't. (Demonstration in this case means a full examination by a competent authority.) Your clients will not see the value of this until you tell them about it. Until they understand the significance of certification, their reaction to the higher rates you charge will range from accusations of overcharging to threats of retaining someone else's services. However, many of these objections go away once you make them aware of the advantages of certification.

The approach you take to this education process depends on the techniques you use to run your business. A hard-sell consultant might want to schedule a meeting with the client to talk about this new certification and to make a proposal based on what it represents. A soft-sell consultant might choose to simply print a brochure that fully explains what certification means and provide it to the client during a scheduled visit. Other consultants might use a combination of approaches or might simply mention it during the course of a regular meeting. Your methods of managing your business determine which techniques feel the most comfortable to you. However, the question of informing the client is clear. If you don't tell your client why your certification is important, then they will never know. An uninformed client is your very worst enemy.

There are specific advantages to each technique for keeping your client informed. For example, brochures can double as advertisement. If a client passes your brochure on to a friend, you might find yourself with a new client. On the other hand, the direct special meeting approach might yield a new networking job. A mention during a regular meeting might improve the intimacy between you and your client. They might feel that you're letting them in on something special. This often translates into greater customer loyalty and support.

You need to consider the temperament of your client when approaching them with news of your certification. Some clients like to talk with a consultant who lets them think about whatever the consultant has to say. They like to take the time required to fully think about what the new

Showing clients what certification means

certification does mean to their business. Other clients might appreciate the hard sell. They take it as a sign that you are an aggressive businessperson when you present your certification quickly and then add a proposal on how they could use the certification within their business. Many retail customers fall into this category. Mentioning it during a meeting with a small business client can really work wonders. A small business needs to maintain the feeling of intimacy rather than the cold business approach used by corporations. Whatever method you use, make sure you take your temperament and that of your client into account before you pursue it.

Determining what to charge

Figuring out what to charge is always a difficult question. Charging too much will yield a dead business when your clients go to your competitor for their networking needs. Charging too little can give you more business but not much profit. You need to find a middle ground between charging too much and too little. Unfortunately this is like one of those psychology tests that we all hate. There are no right answers, just right answers for you. No matter how little you charge, someone who really wants a lower price can probably find it. The same holds true for higher prices. Of course, the people who determine this middle ground are your competitors. Your competitors are the ones who will steal your clients and put you out of business. (Of course, you'll do the same to your competitors given the chance.) The bottom line is if a client sees an opportunity to get the same level of support that you provide from someone else for less, you can be sure that they will use it.

So how do you determine what the middle ground is? You can start by doing a little research. Call the competition to see what they charge. There is no reason for them to withhold the information from you if you call as someone looking for information rather than as a competitor. Another place to look is your local computer magazine or newspaper. Vendors often publish their rates for a specific type of installation.

Sometimes the previous methods don't produce any results. When this happens you can resort to a number of alternative methods to get the information you need. For example, if you have a large enough client base with fairly new LANs, you can always ask them what they paid for the service. Of course, this only helps if you weren't the one installing the LAN. Federal, state, and local governments keep statistics of what businesses charge for certain services. You can find what you need to know from these sources as well.

There are other resources you should consider using. For example, CompuServe and other on-line services host a wide variety of consultant-based forums. You can usually find out the current rate for a given service by polling this group of people. One word of caution here: many of the consultants that frequent these on-line services are at the upper end of the pay scale. You might not get a true reading on what the actual average rate of pay is for a specific service.

As you can see, the only limits on the sources of information you use are the resources you want to tap. Deciding what you want to charge doesn't stop here. You also need to resolve such issues as what to charge for parts. Some consultants don't charge anything at all. They make up for any parts sales by charging a higher hourly rate. Other consultants tack 10 to 15 percent onto the price of the parts they sell and charge a lower hourly rate. Both approaches are equally useful. You need to decide which approach your clients will appreciate more.

There is also the issue of when to apply different rates. Some consultants offer more than one service. You need to decide if you want to charge the same rate for software installation as you do for network maintenance. If you decide to charge one inclusive rate, you might find that some customers balk when you present a bill for training that is the same as their network installation.

If you decide to use different pay scales for different services, you need to decide when one pay scale ends and the other begins. This is one place where consultants can run into trouble. Some clients will try to cheat the consultant by saying that the service they performed should be at a lower rate than the service the consultant actually performed. For example, what happens if the client constantly interrupts you with questions during a network installation. Do you charge them the network installation rate or the lower training rate? The client will choose the training rate. They might not feel you deserve the full networking rate because you spent that time training them. The best course of action is to tell the client what rate you are charging for the work you are performing. Make sure you inform them when the rate changes because the task you are performing changes.

As you can see, rate setting is not the easiest part of consulting. You need to expend the energy required to provide the client with written rates and the methods you use for charging them. You also need to make them aware of when a rate changes and why. If possible, always make sure you write down the rules for rate changes and get the customer's signature. (Many consultants refuse to work without a signed contract; it's very easy to see why.)

Respect—it's not given, it's earned. That is a saying that many of us hear as we advance along our career paths. Yet how many of us really know

Professionalism

what the saying means? Professionalism in the way you perform your job is what earns you the respect of your clients. Professionalism means that you are proud of your abilities and the work you do. It also means that you set certain standards for yourself and stand by the work you do. Some people call this type of behavior old fashioned or out of date, but most clients appreciate a professional when they see one.

Where do you stand on this issue? How do you know when you achieve professional status? Some people set a stiff set of rules and call it professionalism. Nothing could be further from true professionalism than a set of stiff rules. Even crooks and thieves set rules for themselves. They always use the rules as a means to skirt their real responsibility and neglect to fulfill their promises. Professionalism is more a mind-set and less a stiff set of rules than many people think. A professional needs to bend with the changing circumstances of everyday living. Figure 8-3 is a checklist you can use to measure your professional standing.

As you can see, there are many situations where you might need to take time to think about the consequences of your actions before you actually do them. For example, when does a client deserve warranty service rather than paying for a new piece of hardware? There are gray areas that make this a hard question to answer. Yet if you do not answer the question, you might find yourself in a no-win situation. Imagine that a client calls you in for warranty service on a drive that broke during use. If the client appears to have broken the part, you might feel they should pay for it. On the other hand, the client might use the part in the manner prescribed by the vendor. The vendor might make it so poorly that there is no way to use the part without breaking it. What if this is a very expensive part and the vendor has a reputation for not honoring their warranty? (This happens more often than you might think.) If you perform the warranty service, you will lose money on the job. On the other hand, if you don't provide warranty service, you will lose a valuable client.

Perhaps the most difficult part of being a professional is figuring out when actions on your part could prevent a situation from happening at all. For example, in the previous example you might choose to use a higher quality part during installation. The higher quality part should last longer and you won't need to figure out whether to honor your warranty. Because you used a higher quality part, both you and the client are happy with the results. Setting a standard for yourself might lose you a few jobs because you can't compete on cost, but it can prevent you from losing money later when the inexpensive parts break down. Every job has potential risks and paybacks. The professional weighs the cost of each action during a job and chooses the course that produces the best long-term results.

- Use high-quality parts whenever possible. High quality does not necessarily mean high cost. Look for product reviews in trade magazines and newspapers. It also helps to look for opinions from other network professionals on CompuServe or other on-line media.

- Try to reduce costs whenever it will not affect the quality or usefulness of a product the client needs. If a product breaks the first time you use it or the part does not perform the task the client requires, then buying it at discount does not solve any problems. In fact, it actually creates more problems. However, buying a high-priced product simply to get the name value discredits your ability to help the client make prudent buying decisions.

- Always consider the cost of losing a client versus the cost of losing the money from one job. Losing a client always costs you more money than you'll lose from one job. If the client feels you mistreated him/her, find out what it will take to restore confidence. Often this means that you'll lose the profit from a job to save the client's trust.

- Never break the law to meet the demands of an unyielding client. For example, some clients will insist that you install pirated software on their network even though they know such an act is illegal. It is always better to lose a client than to knowingly break the law. Otherwise the client will expect you to break the law as often as they see fit. In addition, you will share in the client's guilt if you get caught performing the illegal act.

8-3
Professional network consultant's business guide.

- Try to honor your warranty whenever possible. Many clients will try to convince you to honor unreasonable interpretations of the warranty you offer as part of your services. It often helps to honor the unreasonable request to maintain the client. Of course, this can backfire if the client starts expecting you to perform this service every time there is a dispute. The most reasonable course of action is to make sure the client understands that you are honoring the unreasonable request in the hope of maintaining a good relationship.

- Use the clearest wording possible in any written documentation you provide the client. This includes contracts and warranties. Make sure you go through the contract or warranty with the client and explain anything they don't understand. Using this technique helps reduce confusion later. It might also prevent you from losing a valued client by reducing the chances of misunderstandings.

- Always perform the work to the best of your ability. Even if the client does not possess the level of technical competance that you do, they do know what task the network should perform when you finish. Make sure that both hardware and software are up to par. Alert the user to potential problems with equipment that you did not install. Help the client understand why there are specific limitations to the installation you create for them.

- Never be afraid to admit that you can't perform a specific task. The client can respect you if you simply say that you can't perform a specific task they need help with. Trying to perform the task when you lack the skills will make the customer less likely to hire you again in the future.

Professionalism is important for another reason. When people see you as a technician certified by Novell to maintain their network, they expect a higher standard of service. After all, you convinced the client to pay you a higher hourly rate based on the assumption that they would receive better service. You are supposed to represent the best the client can get in regard to quality workmanship. Your certification proves that you care more about how people perceive your services than the person who does not choose to get certified. When you are on the job you represent not only yourself, but every other certified individual who follows you.

As you can see, professionalism is not a mere word. It represents a way of doing business and a particular mind-set. There are many "experts" performing network installations today, but few professionals. You need to work to maintain a professional mind-set as your career progresses if you expect people to regard you as something more than a hammer mechanic. Maintaining such a high standard is hard work, but it pays many dividends.

So what will professionalism buy you? It might buy you some peace of mind. Peace of mind might not seem like very much until you face hostile clients a few times. A professional gets a happy greeting from the client every time they go in to do work. The reason is simple, the client knows that the professional will do the very best they can to get the network up and running. More important than a great customer relationship, professionalism will buy you customer loyalty. Customer loyalty translates into regular paychecks with a lot less effort than finding a new client. Every time you have to find a new client, you need to set up a new contract, get to know their installation, and perform a lot of nonpaid work. This really reduces the benefit you see from working for the client. It isn't until you work for the client for a time that the relationship begins to pay off. (This does not mean that one-time jobs are not profitable, it simply means that long-term relationships are more profitable.)

Even if professionalism is old fashioned, people still respect it and look for it whenever possible. They want to know someone who takes the time to get the job done right the first time. Any other course of action is a waste of their time, your time, materials, and it reduces the impact of your certification. Remember, you worked hard to become certified by Novell to do the work you do. Keep up the good work; maintain your professionalism.

Conclusion This chapter was designed to meet the needs of the networking professional. It provides you with all the tools you need to efficiently market your new skills to your current and prospective clients. This is an important part of gaining something from the certification you worked so hard to get.

The first section of this chapter looked at the guerrilla warfare aspect of marketing your certification. How do you get the clients to recognize your new skill without boring them to death? Many consultants find that this is one of the more difficult aspects of selling their certification.

The second section of this chapter talked about the benefits of carrying your identification card. Pride in your work and in your appearance are two of the things that a client looks for in a consultant. Carrying your badge in a conspicuous place not only tells the client that you are a professional, it helps sell your certification. Remember, networking jobs can help you raise the bottom line. Working at a higher rate of pay is always a desirable goal for the networking professional.

The third section of this chapter talked about what you need to do once you get the client interested. This includes everything from deciding what services to offer to telling the client what your certification means. Once you get the client's interest, it's up to you to sell them on the benefits of your certification.

The final section of this chapter helped you determine what your certification means from a business perspective. For example, what do you charge for the new services you want to offer your clients? Trying to charge too much could cost you clients, both current and future. A higher rate of pay also means that you need to address some professionalism concerns. If you are charging the client more, they deserve and expect some side benefits in addition to the main service you provide. Where do you draw the line? What is the level of professionalism you need to maintain to keep your current clients, gain new ones, and still get that pay increase we're all looking for? This section helped you answer these and many other questions.

Important telephone numbers

Novell Main Office: 1-800-453-1267

Novell Education Department fax: 1-801-429-2500

Novell FaxBack: 1-800-233-3382 or 1-801-429-5363

Drake Testing Registration: 1-800-RED-EXAM

Novell Technical Support: 1-800-NET-WARE

Novell Users International (NUI): 1-800-873-3976 or 1-214-419-7882

Novell Education: 1-800-233-EDUC or 1-801-429-5508

Novell After-market Products: 1-800-346-7177 or 1-801-429-7000

Novell Education Materials Order: 1-800-346-6855

Novell Education Area Manager, Western U.S.: 1-408-747-4339

Novell Education Area Manager, West Central U.S.: 1-214-387-7900

Novell Education Area Manager, East Central U.S.: 1-708-228-7676

Novell Education Area Manager, Northeast U.S.: 1-215-647-0664

Novell Education Area Manager, Southeast U.S.: 1-404-698-8350

Novell Education Area Manager, Canada: 1-416-940-2670

CompuServe Registration: See your startup kit for instructions.

Sources of additional information

Computer Technology Review
924 Westwood Blvd., Suite 650
Los Angeles, CA 90024-2910
310-208-1335

Data Communications
1221 Avenue of the Americas
New York, NY 10020
1-800-525-5003

Data Based Advisor
Data Based Solutions, Inc.
4010 Morena Blvd., Suite 200
San Diego, CA 92117
619-483-6400
Fax: 619-483-9851

Hands-On Guide to Network Management
Tab-McGraw Hill
Blue Ridge Summit, PA 17294-0850
1-800-233-1128
ISBN #0-8306-4440-7

LAN Computing
Professional Press, Inc.
101 Witmer Rd.
Horsham, PA 19044
215-957-4269

LAN Technology
P.O. Box 52315
Boulder, CO 80321-2315
1-800-456-1654

LAN Times
Publication Office
1900 O'Farrell St., Suite 200
San Mateo, CA 94403
1-800-525-5003

NetWare Application Notes
Novell
122 E. 1700 S.
Provo, UT 84606
1-800-377-4136
303-297-2725

NetWare Buyers Guide
Novell
122 E. 1700 S.
Provo, UT 84606-6194
1-800-873-2831

NetWare Solutions
DB Media Publications, Inc.
10711 Burnet Rd., Suite 305
Austin, TX 78758
512-873-7761
Fax: 512-873-7782

Network Computing
CMP Publications
600 Community Dr.
Manhasset, NY 11030
1-516-562-5071

Network News
CNE Professional Association
Mail Stop E-31-1
122 E. 1700 S.
Provo, UT 84606-6194
1-800-926-3776

Network World
161 Worcester Rd.
Framingham, MA 01701-9172
1-508-820-7444

PC Magazine
Ziff-Davis Publishing Co.
One Park Avenue
New York, NY 10016
212-503-5255

PC Novice
Reed Corporation
120 West Harvest Dr.
P.O. Box 85380
Lincoln, NE 68501
1-800-544-1264

Systems Integration
Cahners Publishing Associates/
Reed Publishing (USA), Inc.
275 Washington St.
Newton, MA 02158
617-964-3030
Fax: 617-558-4506

Course descriptions

The NetWare 2.2 System Manager course teaches you the fundamentals of managing and maintaining a Novell 2.2 network. This course is for the person who is a system administrator, backup system administrator, or a beginner who wants to learn more about the workings of NetWare. Topics covered in this class include

NetWare 2.2 System Manager

- NetWare hardware and software basics,
- NetWare directory structures,
- drive mappings,
- NetWare security,
- NetWare console and command line utilities,
- NetWare menu utilities,
- basic printing,
- creating and using login scripts,
- creating Novell menus, and
- loading applications.

This course includes instructor-led lectures and hands-on exercises. The hands-on exercises follow the same steps and procedures used in setting up and maintaining networks for real companies.

The prerequisites for this class require the student to have a basic working knowledge of DOS and an understanding of basic LAN concepts. The student's understanding of DOS must include directory hierarchy, how to create directories, creating ASCII files, copying files, deleting files, and changing directories.

Course length: 3 days
Course number: 501
Test number: 50-20
Number of credits: 3

NetWare 2.2 Advanced System Manager

The NetWare 2.2 Advanced System Manager course covers the advanced management features of Novell NetWare 2.2. The target audience of this course is the person who manages an existing NetWare 2.2 network or a consultant needing advanced information about the NetWare 2.2 operating system. Topics covered in this course include

- NetWare 2.2 installation overview,
- NetWare accounting,
- advanced printing,
- advanced menu utilities,
- performance management,
- troubleshooting network problems, and
- memory management.

This course includes instructor-led lectures and structured hands-on lab exercises. The lectures and lab exercises enhance the student's understanding of the tasks and duties performed daily by system administrators and consultants working in the field of networking.

Prerequisites for this class include a working knowledge of DOS and NetWare. In addition, you must attend the NetWare 2.2 System Manager course before attending this course. The pace of the course is quite fast, making prior knowledge of NetWare a necessity.

Course length: 2 days
Course number: 502
Test number: 50-44
Number of credits: 2

NetWare 3.11 System Manager

The NetWare 3.11 System Manager course centers on the basic tasks and duties of the administrator that is using the Novell NetWare 3.11 operating system. Intended audiences for this course include network managers and networking consultants. This course teaches you the basics of using, managing, and maintaining a network running NetWare 3.11. Topics covered in this course include

- NetWare 3.11 basics,
- setting up directory structures,

- working with NetWare drive mappings,
- understanding and implementing NetWare security,
- menu utilities for administrators,
- file server administration utilities,
- network printing,
- customizing users' access and use to the network,
- managing network applications, and
- using Novell's backup utility.

This course includes instructor-led lectures and hands-on exercises. The hands-on exercises follow the same steps and procedures used in setting up and maintaining networks for real companies.

The prerequisites for this class include a basic working knowledge of DOS and an understanding of basic LAN concepts. The student's understanding of DOS must include the directory hierarchy, how to create and manage directories, creating ASCII files, copying files, and deleting files.

Course length: 3 days
Course number: 505
Test number: 50-91
Number of credits: 3

NetWare 3.11 Advanced System Manager

The Novell NetWare 3.11 Advanced System Manager course is an extension of the NetWare 3.11 System Manager course. The lectures and lab exercises enhance the student's understanding of the tasks and duties performed daily by system administrators and consultants working in the field of networking. Intended audience for this course includes system administrators and consultants. These advanced features include printing and the art of fine-tuning the network. Other topics covered in the course include

- advanced command line and menu utilities,
- concepts and procedures of performance management,
- advanced setup and troubleshooting of network printing,
- NetWare's remote management utilities,
- concepts and procedures of open protocol support, and
- NetWare's prevention and maintenance utilities.

This course includes instructor-led lectures and structured hands-on lab exercises. The lectures and lab exercises enhance the actual tasks and duties performed by system administrators and consultants working in the field of networking.

Prerequisites for this class include having a working knowledge of DOS and NetWare. In addition, you must attend the NetWare 3.11 System

Manager course before attending this course. The pace of the course is quite fast, making prior knowledge of NetWare a necessity.

Course length: 2 days
Course number: 515
Test number: 50-82
Number of credits: 2

NetWare 4.0 Administration

The NetWare 4.0 Administration course teaches you the fundamental knowledge and skills to manage and administer a Novell NetWare 4.0 network. This course is for the person that currently manages or plans to manage a network running NetWare 4.0 or a consultant planning to support the operating system. Topics covered in this course include

- introduction of NetWare 4.0,
- connecting to and using NetWare 4.0 resources,
- NetWare directory services (NDS),
- NetWare 4.0 file system,
- file system security,
- directory services security,
- NetWare 4.0 file server management,
- introduction to printing, and
- setting up the users' network environment.

This course includes instructor-led lectures and hands-on exercises. The hands-on exercises follow the same steps and procedures used in setting up and maintaining networks for real companies.

The prerequisites for this class include a basic working knowledge of DOS and an understanding of basic LAN concepts. The student's understanding of DOS must include the directory hierarchy, how to create and manage directories, creating ASCII files, copying files, and deleting files. The student should also have a working understanding of Windows 3.0 or above.

Course length: 4 days
Course number: 520
Test number: 50-122
Number of credits: 3

NetWare 4.0 Advanced Administration

The NetWare 4.0 Advanced Administration course continues where the NetWare 4.0 Administration course stops. This course is for the manager or consultant working with a complex network installation. The course teaches you about planning, implementing, fine-tuning, and overseeing a complex network using NetWare 4.0. Topics covered in this course include

- an introduction to complex Novell networks,
- planning and managing the NetWare directory services (NDS),
- advanced security features,
- resource auditing features,
- advanced printing,
- managing client and network features and services, and
- fine-tuning NetWare 4.0 for optimum performance.

This course includes instructor-led lectures and hands-on exercises. The hands-on exercises follow the same steps and procedures used in setting up and maintaining networks for real companies.

Prerequisites for this class include having a working knowledge of DOS and NetWare. In addition, you must attend the NetWare 4.0 Administration course before attending this course. The pace of this course is quite fast, making prior knowledge of NetWare a necessity. The student's understanding of DOS must include the directory hierarchy, how to create and manage directories, creating ASCII files, copying files, and deleting files. The student should also have a working understanding of Windows 3.0 or above.

Course length: 3 days
Course number: 525
Test number: 50-123
Number of credits: 2

NetWare 3.11 to 4.0 Update

The NetWare 3.11 to 4.0 Update course identifies the new and enhanced features of the NetWare 4.0 operating system over the NetWare 3.11 operating system. The course is for the person who has experience working with networks, especially NetWare 3.11. This includes system administrators and consultants. Combining this course with the NetWare Installation and Configuration Workshop course offers a complete overview of NetWare 4.0. Topics covered in this course include

- NetWare 4.0 overview,
- NetWare directory services (NDS) concepts and implementation,
- NetWare 4.0 security for NDS and the file system,
- client and utility changes,
- NetWare 4.0 print services,
- resource auditing services, and
- storage management features and services.

This course includes instructor-led lectures and hands-on exercises. The hands-on exercises follow the same steps and procedures used in setting up and maintaining networks for real companies.

The prerequisites for this class include prior NetWare experience (preferably with NetWare 3.11). Also required is a basic working knowledge of DOS and an understanding of basic LAN concepts. The student's understanding of DOS must include the directory hierarchy, how to create and manage directories, creating ASCII files, copying files, and deleting files. The student should also have a working understanding of Windows 3.0 or above.

Course length: 3 days
Course number: 526
Test number: 50-124
Number of credits: 2

NetWare 4.0 Installation and Configuration Workshop

The NetWare 4.0 Installation and Configuration Workshop teaches the student how to plan and install the NetWare 4.0 operating system and client workstations. This course is for the person who has prior NetWare experience and whose duties include managing or maintaining a network. This includes system managers and consultants. Combining this course with the NetWare 3.11 to 4.0 Update course provides a complete understanding of NetWare 4.0. Topics covered in this course include

- installing the 4.0 operating system,
- installing the DOS and Windows workstation client,
- migrating from NetWare 3.11 to NetWare 4.0,
- managing the NetWare directory services (NDS),
- setting up NetWare printing services,
- backing up and restoring data using NetWare utilities, and
- managing the file server using new NetWare utilities.

This course includes some instructor-led lectures with most of the course consisting of hands-on exercises. The hands-on exercises follow the same steps and procedures used in setting up and maintaining networks for real companies.

The prerequisites for this class include prior NetWare experience (preferably with NetWare 3.11). Also required is a basic working knowledge of DOS and an understanding of basic LAN concepts. The student's understanding of DOS must include the directory hierarchy, how to create and manage directories, creating ASCII files, copying files, and deleting files. The student should also have a working understanding of Windows 3.0 or above.

Course length: 2 days
Course number: 804
Test number: 50-126
Number of credits: 2

The NetWare Service and Support course teaches the student various hardware topics related to installing and maintaining the NetWare operating system. During this course you will install and configure network interface cards and disk subsystems, connect cables, and install both NetWare 2.x and 3.x. Other topics covered in the course include

NetWare Service and Support

- NetWare 2.x architecture,
- NetWare 3.x architecture,
- multiserver networks,
- internetworks,
- network addressing,
- network board configurations,
- network cabling,
- disk storage,
- workstation installation,
- NetWare 2.x and 3.x installation,
- NetWare router installation,
- NetWare upgrading procedures,
- troubleshooting techniques and tools,
- Novell diagnostic utilities, and
- common network problems.

This course is instructor-led, with the students performing many hands-on exercises. The information and exercises in this course are the same tasks that technicians perform on a daily basis.

The prerequisites for this class include the student having a working knowledge of the Intel-based personal computer. Other beneficial prerequisites include a knowledge of LAN and DOS basics.

Course length: 5 days
Course number: 701
Test number: 50-46
Number of credits: 5

The Networking Technologies course provides in-depth instruction that covers the theory and protocols of networking. Discussed in this class are the seven layers of the OSI model, the applications of each layer, and how they relate to networking. The course also contains information about the communication protocols of Novell's IPX/SPX and the TCP/IP protocol used by UNIX. Other topics and technologies covered in this course include

Networking Technologies

- understanding the history of networking,
- the standards setting committees,
- data encoding schemes,

- data transmission modes,
- signal multiplexing and signal conversion,
- network topologies,
- circuit, message, and packet switching techniques,
- the PSTN network,
- functions of the IEEE 802.3, 802.4, and 802.5 standards,
- LocalTalk and AppleTalk technology,
- the SDLC and HDLC protocols used by mainframe networks,
- NetWare protocols of IPX/SPX,
- internet protocols of TCP, UDP, and IP, and
- SNA and DNA network architectures.

This course is lecture only with no hands-on computer exercises. However, the manuals provide written exercises at the end of each of the 29 chapters. The course covers many subjects related to networking in just three days. In comparison to this intensive training, a college course usually covers less material in one year.

The prerequisites for this class are a basic understanding of LANs and a strong desire to learn more about the theories of networking. Because this course covers so much material, from the general to the specific, there is no other Novell-offered course that offers much assistance.

Course length: 3 days
Course number: 200
Test number: 50-80
Number of credits: 3

Sample tests

Throughout this book you have been given many tips and insights on how to prepare for the certification exams. The chapters also include in-depth information about the course outlines, how to attend the courses, and detailed information about which courses are necessary to help you obtain your certification. To fully prepare for the exams, you should also know what the questions will look like.

This appendix introduces you to the types of questions you will see when you take the exams to become Novell certified. The intent of these questions is to help you prepare yourself for the exams by showing you what the questions will look like. It is not our intent to create questions exactly the same as the ones on the tests, although some of them might be similar.

Each section of this appendix starts with a brief paragraph containing some test-taking tips to help you pass the exams. Also contained in the opening paragraph are some of the traps to watch for that Novell has put into the test questions. After each tips and traps paragraph are a series of questions written about the core exams. As you take each of the tests, read the questions carefully. You will find the correct answers for each set of test questions at the end of this appendix. If you want more sample test questions, Novell offers a computer-based program containing sample test questions from many of the CNE, ECNE, and CNI exams. To

Introduction

receive a copy of this program, contact the Novell education department for a diskette or download the program from the NetWire forum on CompuServe.

When taking the test in general, read the test questions and answers completely. Many times you will find the word "not" used to create a reverse logic question. This type of question will have a correct answer for both ways of reading the question, with or without the word "not." Another problem you will find with the test questions is that they are poorly worded or phrased or very ambiguous, in that you really do not understand what they are looking for. When you find these types of questions, try to reason out the answer by applying each answer to the question and finding the one that feels right. Similarly you will find that for some of the questions every answer could be correct; in these cases put on your Novell red glasses and choose the one that Novell recommends from the student manuals.

DOS/ Microcomputer Hardware

The DOS/Microcomputer Hardware exam covers the basic and intermediate concepts pertaining to DOS commands and hardware knowledge. Things to watch for in the DOS section include understanding the configuration files and what command goes in each one, DOS external command syntax, DOS internal command syntax, and knowing how DOS interfaces with input, output, and storage devices. The hardware section of the test covers topics such as the history of computers, processors, memory, storage devices, input and output devices, video, and a general knowledge of the Apple Macintosh and Intel-based computers.

Sample DOS/ Microcomputer Hardware test questions

1. Which microprocessor was developed first?
    A. 8088
    B. 80286
    C. 80386
    D. 80486

2. To warm boot a computer you must
    A. Turn the machine off then back on while it is still warm.
    B. Press the reset button.
    C. Press the CTRL, ALT, and DEL keys all at the same time.
    D. Use the setup disk.

3. Personal computers work with data in which format?
    A. ASCII
    B. Binary
    C. English
    D. Hexadecimal

4. The second set of 128 ASCII characters is known as

   A. ASCII-II.
   B. EBCDIC.
   C. Unix.
   D. Extended character set.

5. To set the time on a personal computer you can

   A. Use the DOS time command.
   B. Use the set time command.
   C. Power the computer off.
   D. It cannot be done.

6. The last drive statement is placed in the _____ file.

   A. Autoexec.bat
   B. Config.sys
   C. Command.com
   D. Either A or B

7. The DOS path command is used to

   A. Tell DOS where to look for files.
   B. Instruct DOS how to run programs.
   C. Instruct DOS which circuit paths to use.
   D. All of the above.

8. One of the purposes for creating directories is

   A. It's fun.
   B. It's mandatory.
   C. It's the only way to run programs.
   D. To help organize your files.

9. Legal DOS wildcard characters consist of _____ and _____.

   A. *, ?
   B. *, !
   C. ?, &
   D. ., :

10. The maximum length of a DOS file name is

   A. 7
   B. 9
   C. 11
   D. 13

The NetWare 2.2 System Manager exams normally contain many questions about the security structure and how it works. Because this is

NetWare 2.2 System Manager

one of the most important parts of NetWare, it makes sense that Novell would spend a lot of time and ask many questions in this area. Other areas of focus in the exam include questions about drive pointers, login scripts, menu utilities, and printing.

When taking the Netware 2.2 and Netware 3.11 System Manager exams, keep in mind which operating system you are taking the test for. Many of the questions are generic so that Novell can use them for either the 2.2 or 3.11 operating system. The set of answers for each question will also be correct for both operating systems. The correct answer is the one that has to do with the test you are taking.

Sample
NetWare 2.2
System Manager
test questions

1. A NetWare 2.2 dedicated file server can utilize a maximum of _____ of RAM.
   A. 8 Mb
   B. 12 Mb
   C. 16 Mb
   D. 255 Mb

2. The NetWare operating system resides at the _____ and controls the _____ devices.
   A. File server, Shared
   B. Workstation, Local
   C. File server, Workstation
   D. Both A and B

3. Which is not a system created directory?
   A. The ETC directory
   B. The System directory
   C. The Public directory
   D. The Login directory

4. Which of the following is the correct MAP syntax?
   A. MAP S2:=FS1/SYS:PUBLIC/DOS
   B. MAP S3:FS1\VOL1\APPS\DB
   C. MAP G:=FS1\SYS;USERS\BOB
   D. MAP S2:=SYS:VOL1:PUBLIC\DOS

5. The NetWare security feature has _____ type(s) of security that is implemented at _____ levels.
   A. 4, 3
   B. 1, 3
   C. 1, 4
   D. None of the above

6. Which of the following access rights are not assigned to a user?

    A. Normal
    B. Read
    C. Erase
    D. Access control

7. The file attributes of SRO is the abbreviation for

    A. System Read/Open.
    B. Shareable Read/Open.
    C. Shareable Read/Only.
    D. System Read/Only.

8. In NetWare you have the capability to create three types of operators; they are _____, _____, and _____.

    A. Console, Print Queue, Print Server
    B. Print Queue, Print Server, System
    C. System, Print Services, Back-up
    D. Print Queue, Print Server, Back-up

9. To print to a printer that is attached directly to the file server, you must

    A. Load the Pserver NLM at the file server.
    B. Load the Pserver EXE file at the file server.
    C. Link the core printing services during the installation of the operating system.
    D. None of the above.

10. What are the three types of login scripts in order of execution?

    A. User, System, Network
    B. Default, System, User
    C. System, User, Default
    D. User, System, Default

NetWare 2.2 Advanced System Manager

The NetWare 2.2 Advanced System Manager exam focuses mainly on the areas of printing, troubleshooting, managing the network, and utilities that will help streamline the setup of the network. Topics that require the most attention and study by most people are printing and the meaning of the statistics in FConsole. Both of these areas are very important topics pertaining to networking in the real world. Without the proper understanding of how to properly use and work with them, you will find yourself in a real quandary.

You will find that many of the test questions relate to real-world situations. The more trouble people have with a particular topic on their network, the more Novell wants to be sure that anyone that they certify knows how to handle the problem. Keeping this in mind, you can better prepare yourself for the exams by studying the most difficult areas of networking.

1. The minimum and maximum amounts of RAM a nondedicated file server can effectively address are
    A. 2.5 Mb and 8 Mb.
    B. 2.5 Mb and 12 Mb.
    C. 2 Mb and no limit.
    D. 2.5 Mb and 16 Mb.

2. What is not an option on the NetWare installation menu?
    A. Basic Installation
    B. Advanced Installation
    C. Maintain Existing System
    D. Transfer from another Server

3. What is not a valid type of workstation shell file?
    A. Netx.com
    B. EMSnetx.exe
    C. XMSnetx.exe
    D. LIMnetx.exe

4. What is the NetWare utility that is used to create the interface between the workstation and the network interface card and what is the file name that is created?
    A. Shgen, Netx.com
    B. WSgen, Netx.com
    C. Shgen, IPX.com
    D. WSgen, IPX.com

5. A NetWare router will not work in which of the following modes?
    A. Dedicated protected mode
    B. Dedicated real mode
    C. Nondedicated protected mode
    D. None of the above

6. The NetWare accounting utility stores all of its entries in which file?
    A. NET$REC.DAT
    B. NET$ACCT.DAT
    C. ACCOUNT$.DAT
    D. Both A and B

7. The makeuser program is an alternative to which NetWare utility?
    A. SYSCON
    B. FILER

C. USER
D. CREATE

8. The D group memory segment is the most important part of the file server memory block. Adding more RAM to the file server increases the amount of this D group memory space.

   A. True
   B. False

9. The FConsole utility can be used by all users of the network.

   A. True
   B. False

10. The FConsole utility is also known as NetWare's _____ utility.

    A. Virtual console
    B. Friendly
    C. D-bug
    D. All of the above

11. The _____ memory pools of NetWare 2.2 can be viewed in the _____ screen of FConsole.

    A. 4, Statistic Summary
    B. 3, Statistic Summary
    C. 3, Memory Summary
    D. 4, Memory Usage

12. By caching data into file server memory, you can increase data access speeds by as much as _____ times.

    A. 10
    B. 30
    C. 50
    D. 100

13. The NetWare print services program can be loaded onto a

    A. File Server.
    B. Workstation.
    C. Router.
    D. All of the above.

14. Print services are automatically set up during installation of the operating system.

    A. True
    B. False

15. Which NetWare utility is used to set up basic network printing?
    A. fINTDEF
    B. PCONSOLE
    C. PRINTCON
    D. PSC

NetWare 3.11 System Manager

The NetWare 3.11 System Manager exam is very similar to the Netware 2.2 System Manager exam. Subjects that demand extra study time include the concepts of NetWare, security, menu utilities, drive mappings, the proper mapping command syntax, and automating the login process with the use of login scripts. Of these topics, security is the one to pay the most attention to. Make sure that you know how the trustee rights, directory rights, and file rights affect each other and how to implement them. You also need a comprehensive understanding of the concepts of attributes (both at the file and directory level), and how to assign them.

The same types of questions will appear on this test as from the 2.2 system manager test. Remember that the only difference between the 2.2 answers and the 3.11 answers is the test that you are taking. In other words, the question will not specify the operating system and the answer will have the correct answer for both NetWare 2.2 and Netware 3.11. Because you are taking the test for 3.11, the correct answer will be the one that deals with the 3.11 operating system.

Sample NetWare 3.11 System Manager test questions

1. NetWare 3.11 does not support which one of the following operating systems?
    A. DOS
    B. UNIX
    C. MACINTOSH
    D. WINDOWS
    E. None of the above

2. The NetWare operating system supports _____ of RAM and _____ of disk storage.
    A. 4 Gb, 32 Tb
    B. 12 Mb, 2 Gb
    C. 16 Mb, 2 Gb
    D. 255 Mb, 4 Gb

3. There are _____ letters available for assignment as network regular drive pointers.
    A. 5
    B. 16

C. 21
D. 26
E. No limit

4. Each NetWare user can have _____ search drive assignments.

   A. 5
   B. 16
   C. 21
   D. 26
   E. No limit

5. NetWare 3.11 has _____ levels of security.

   A. 2
   B. 3
   C. 4
   D. None of the above

6. Which of the following is not a NetWare bindery file?

   A. NET$OBJ.SYS
   B. NET$PROP.SYS
   C. NET$BIND.SYS
   D. NET$VAL.SYS

7. Which of the following are not allowed to create user accounts on the network.

   A. Workgroup managers
   B. User account managers
   C. Supervisor
   D. Supervisor equivalent

8. The modify security right allows a user to change a file's

   A. Contents.
   B. Security rights.
   C. Attributes.
   D. All of the above.

9. If a user is explicitly granted the RF rights to a directory, but the directory has had the R and W rights removed, what are the user's effective rights for that directory?

   A. RW
   B. RF
   C. F
   D. No rights

10. NetWare attribute security can be assigned to

    A. Only files.
    B. Files and directories.
    C. Files and users.
    D. All of the above.

11. When using the NetWare menu utilities, the F3 key will _____ an entry.

    A. Modify
    B. Delete
    C. Mark or toggle
    D. Insert

12. The SYSCON utility can be used to

    A. Create a new user account.
    B. Create a new group account.
    C. Change file attributes.
    D. Both A and B.
    E. All of the above.

13. NetWare console commands are divided into the four categories of

    A. Screen, configuration, maintenance, and installation.
    B. Installation, maintenance, load, and bind.
    C. Down, load, bind, and monitor.
    D. Configuration, maintenance, installation, and monitor.

14. The user login script runs from the _____ file which is located in the _____ directory.

    A. Login.exe, user's mail
    B. User$log, mail
    C. Personal, user's home
    D. Login, user's mail

15. When creating a NetWare menu, the script file must have a _____ extension.

    A. .SPT
    B. .MNU
    C. .EXE
    D. .DAT

16. The NetWare utility to backup and restore DOS and Macintosh files on a 2.x and 3.x file server, is the _____ utility.

    A. SBackup
    B. Narchive

C. NBackup

D. None of the above

The Netware 3.11 Advanced System Manager exam deals quite a bit with the management strategies and performance management of the operating system. Many of the questions on the test deal with how to set up workstation files such as the standard IPX and NETX interface as well as the ODI shells, the shell enhancement configuration files of NET.CFG and SHELL.CFG, and the commands that go into them. You will also find the performance management and advanced printing section of the student manual receive heavy emphasis during the exam. Remember that these are the areas that give the most grief to network administrators, so Novell wants to make sure that you fully comprehend the concepts and use of each area. Another area that generates quite a few questions is the prevention and maintenance sections. This area has some very good information about general maintenance and prevention strategies for your networks. This section also covers the SBACKUP utility. You can count on having a question or two about SBACKUP.

1. The NetWare command line utility that can list all the files and the location of each file for a specific user is

    A. DIR.
    B. LISTDIR.
    C. FILEFIND.
    D. NDIR.

2. At the workstation, a user can modify the shell files by using a _____ file.

    A. Config.sys
    B. Net.cfg
    C. Net.sys
    D. Shell.sys

3. The shell.cfg and net.cfg file will modify

    A. IPX.com.
    B. Netx.com.
    C. Command.com.
    D. Both A and B.

4. To automatically start the file server monitor utility during the server startup, you would place the appropriate command into the _____ file.

    A. Config.sys
    B. Startup.ncf

C. Autoexec.bat

D. Autoexec.ncf

5. The secure console command would prevent anyone from doing the following

    A. Loading NLMs from the C drive.

    B. Entering the operating system debugger.

    C. Loading DOS after the file server has been downed.

    D. All of the above.

6. NetWare uses which tables to locate files on the hard disk?

    A. File allocation

    B. Directory entry

    C. File location

    D. Both A and B

7. On a file server with multiple volumes, the DET is located

    A. Only on volume SYS.

    B. On the C drive.

    C. On any volume the installer specifies.

    D. On each volume.

8. The Directory entry table holds information about

    A. Files.

    B. Directories.

    C. File trustees.

    D. All of the above.

9. Disk allocation blocks can be divided into _____ block size for each volume.

    A. 4k

    B. 32k

    C. 64k

    D. All of the above

10. If the disk allocation blocks are set to 4k on one volume and 16k on another volume, then the file cache buffers should be set to _____ in size.

    A. 4k

    B. 8k

    C. 12k

    D. 16k

    E. Any of the above

11. File server memory that is not used by the operating system or DOS is given to the _____ pool.

    A. File cache buffer
    B. Permanent memory
    C. Allocate memory
    D. System reserve memory

12. If total cache buffers fall to _____ percent or below, you should add more RAM immediately to the file server.

    A. 10
    B. 20
    C. 50
    D. 80

13. NetWare printing performance is affected by

    A. The number of print jobs.
    B. The size of print jobs.
    C. The number of printers.
    D. All of the above.

14. If changes are made to an existing print server setup, the changes will take effect

    A. Immediately.
    B. The next day.
    C. After the file server is downed.
    D. The next time the print server is brought up.

15. The NetWare remote management feature allows the system manager to allow a workstation to act as the file server console.

    A. True
    B. False

16. The NetWare name space allows non-DOS operating systems to

    A. Store files in native format.
    B. Retain file names longer than 11 characters.
    C. Retain file attributes.
    D. All of the above.
    E. None of the above.

17. The NetWare SBackup utility will

    A. Back up 2.x and 3.x file servers.
    B. Be run from a workstation with a tape unit attached to it.
    C. Only be used from the file server.
    D. Only back up UNIX files.

18. The SBackup utility creates temporary files in the _____ directory during the backup process.
    A. Public
    B. System
    C. Mail
    D. ETC

19. Before running the VRepair utility, you must first
    A. Get written permission from Novell.
    B. Log every user out of the network.
    C. Dismount the volume.
    D. Down the file server.

20. At the file server, the track on command is used to
    A. Turn on the router tracking screen.
    B. Track what each user does on the network.
    C. Track disk usage.
    D. None of the above.

NetWare Service and Support

The Netware Service and Support exam questions are fairly straightforward. This is a hands-on class that deals with physically installing the network, from the cable to the operating system, and troubleshooting problems on the network. Study the sections on multiserver networks and internetworks. Know the specifications for each of the cable types listed in the book (yes, they might ask you the minimum allowable amount of cable between nodes in a 10base2 network, with the answer in either feet or meters). Also memorize the options that are on the installation screens for NetWare 2.15, 2.2, and 3.11. You must also know the minimum hardware requirements for each of the operating systems as well as for the workstations. This is one exam where it really helps if you can install the operating systems many times before taking the exam. You will find that this course and manual also covers the NetWare repair utilities. If you take the course you should use them at least once. Chances are high that there will be questions about their use and functions.

Sample NetWare Service and Support test questions

1. If a single network has more than one file server on the same physical cabling system, it is known as a
    A. Multiserver network.
    B. Internetwork.
    C. One-cable network.
    D. Both and A and B.

2. The network address has a maximum length of _____ digits.
    A. 6

B. 8
C. 12
D. 16

3. Each workstation on the network must be assigned a _____ address.

    A. I/O
    B. Office
    C. Node
    D. Video

4. When using thin net ethernet cabling, each trunk segment must not exceed

    A. 3035 feet.
    B. 925 meters.
    C. 185 meters.
    D. 2000 feet.

5. NetWare's hot fix feature is used to

    A. Remove NICs from the computer while it is running.
    B. Physically repair hard disk drives.
    C. Watch for bad data blocks during writes.
    D. Repair NetWare volumes.

6. WSgen is used to create what file?

    A. Netx.com
    B. Net.cfg
    C. IPXODI.com
    D. IPX.com

7. During the install process of NetWare 2.2, the ztest utility will

    A. Erase all data on the disk.
    B. Not effect data on the disk.
    C. Test the network adapter.
    D. Test the entire disk for bad blocks.

8. To create an internal router in NetWare 2.2 you must

    A. Select more than one network adapter during the operating system generation.
    B. Use the BRgen software.
    C. Use the Routegen software.
    D. Use the Introute software.

9. To install NetWare 2.15 you would use the _____ utility.

    A. Install.exe
    B. Server.exe

C. Netgen.exe

D. Sysgen.exe

10. To upgrade a file server from NetWare 2.x to 3.x using the transfer method, you must have

A. Two file servers.

B. Two networks.

C. Two supervisors.

D. A tape drive.

11. The first step in network troubleshooting is to

A. Take corrective action.

B. Bill the customer.

C. Complete the presite planning checklist.

D. Test every assembly on the network.

12. When talking to a person who is giving you information about a network problem, you should

A. Buy them lunch.

B. Ask general questions, so as not to intimidate them.

C. Talk to their supervisor.

D. Ask isolating questions.

13. To repair the NetWare bindery files, you would use the _____ utility.

A. Vrepair

B. Syscon

C. Dconfig

D. Bindfix

14. NetWire is Novell's technical BBS.

A. True

B. False

15. When using the Dconfig utility, it is possible to add another LAN driver to the operating system.

A. True

B. False

Networking Technologies

This is the most difficult exam you will take. The course covers 29 chapters in just three days. The information from this course is not Novell-specific, so those of you with years of NetWare experience plan to burn the midnight oil in preparation for this exam. The best advice for helping you to pass this exam is to memorize the student manual and learn as many of the acronyms as possible. The course and manual are so in-depth that there is not any one single section or topic that is more important than any other. Take the test immediately after you study the manuals so that you have less time to forget anything you have just read. If you fail the exam the first time don't get discouraged—almost everyone who takes the test fails it the first time. Use it as a learning tool for the next time you take the test. Write down all the questions you can remember immediately after the test. Use these questions as a study guide for the next time. Chances are you won't have the same test questions, but you will get a feel for what Novell is expecting.

1. At layer five of the OSI reference model is the _____ layer, which is located between the layers of _____ and _____.

   A. Session, application, presentation
   B. Session, transport, presentation
   C. Network, transport, session
   D. Network, data-link, session

Sample Networking Technologies test questions

2. All vendors are OSI compliant.

   A. True
   B. False

3. The U.S. representative to the ISO is

   A. ANSI.
   B. IEEE.
   C. IBM.
   D. Novell.

4. In an analog signal the _____ is the measurement from the reference line to the top of the wave.

   A. Frequency
   B. Phase
   C. Curl
   D. Amplitude

5. In a TTY interface or PC that is TTY compatible, the encoding scheme that is typically used is

   A. Return to zero.
   B. Unipolar.
   C. Biphase.
   D. Manchester.

6. Base band transmission systems use

   A. Digital signals.
   B. Analog signals.

C. TV signals.
D. Both A and B.

7. An example of a DTE is a

A. Modem.
B. PC.
C. Codec.
D. Telephone.

8. Asynchronous transmission uses start and stop bits to synchronize the signal. This clocking only needs to be accurate for _____ to _____ ticks.

A. 1, 2
B. 2, 5
C. 8, 14
D. 18, 24

9. Two of the most common token passing LAN standards are

A. IEEE 802.4 and 802.5.
B. 10baseT and Token Ring.
C. Arcnet and Ethernet.
D. Ethernet and Token Ring.

10. Repeaters operate at the _____ layer of the OSI reference model.

A. Physical
B. Data-link
C. Network
D. Transport

11. Gateways use which layers of the OSI reference model?

A. Application
B. Transport
C. Session
D. All of the above

12. HDLC, SDLC, and LAPB are all examples of protocols that operate at the _____ layer of the OSI model.

A. Application
B. Transport
C. Data-link
D. Session

13. The IEEE project 802 is mainly concerned with what two layers of the OSI model?

A. Application and presentation

B. Network and transport
C. Network and data-link
D. Data-link and physical

14. If you wanted to get information on broad band technology, which IEEE committee would you talk to?

   A. 802.1
   B. 802.6
   C. 802.7
   D. 802.8

15. In an 802.5 environment, how many bytes does the token consist of?

   A. 1
   B. 2
   C. 3
   D. 4

16. Arcnet uses a _____ protocol.

   A. Character-oriented
   B. Byte-oriented
   C. Hybrid
   D. Contention-oriented

17. In a local talk frame, the FCS is calculated on all fields except

   A. The flags.
   B. The abort sequence.
   C. Both A and B.
   D. None of the above.

18. The Internet protocol provides _____, _____ delivery of packets.

   A. Connectionless, nonguaranteed
   B. Connectionless, guaranteed
   C. Connected, nonguaranteed
   D. Connected, guaranteed

19. The SNA reference model includes _____ layers.

   A. 4
   B. 5
   C. 7
   D. 9

20. Above the _____ layer of the OSI reference model, DNA permits two access modes.

   A. Transport
   B. Session

C. Network

D. Data-link

Sample test answers

Listed below are the answers to the sample test questions. There is room next to each answer so that you can write notes about each question or list the page number where you found the answers.

**DOS/
Microcomputer
Hardware**

1. A
2. C
3. B
4. D
5. A
6. B
7. A
8. D
9. A
10. C

**NetWare 2.2
System Manager**

1. B
2. A
3. A
4. A
5. A
6. A
7. C
8. A
9. C
10. C

**NetWare 2.2
Advanced System
Manager**

1. A
2. D
3. D
4. D
5. D
6. A
7. A
8. B
9. A

10. A
11. A
12. D
13. D
14. B
15. B

1. E
2. A
3. D
4. B
5. C
6. C
7. B
8. C
9. B
10. B
11. A
12. D
13. A
14. D
15. B
16. C

NetWare 3.11
System Manager

1. D
2. B
3. D
4. D
5. D
6. D
7. D
8. D
9. D
10. A
11. A
12. B
13. D

NetWare 3.11
Advanced System
Manager

14. D
15. A
16. D
17. C
18. B
19. C
20. A

NetWare Service and Support

1. A
2. B
3. C
4. C
5. C
6. D
7. A
8. A
9. C
10. A
11. C
12. D
13. D
14. A
15. B

Networking Technologies

1. B
2. B
3. A
4. D
5. B
6. A
7. B
8. C
9. A
10. A
11. D
12. C

13. D
14. C
15. C
16. A
17. C
18. A
19. C
20. A

Glossary

ACS *See* asynchronous communications server.

ad-hoc solution   A technique for solving an event or problem that requires an immediate solution. It usually refers to something that is not planned, but implemented without consideration of any side effects. For example, an ad-hoc report solves the need to present information in a specific manner without programming that report into the application that prepares it.

ASCII   American Standard Code for Information Interchange. A standard method of equating the numeric representations available in a computer to human readable form. For example, the number 32 represents a space. There are 128 characters (7 bits) in the standard ASCII code. The extended ASCII code uses 8 bits for 256 characters. Display adapters from the same machine type usually use the same upper 128 characters. Printers, however, might reserve these upper 128 characters for nonstandard characters. For example, many Epson printers use them for the italic representation of the lower 128 characters.

asynchronous communications server (ACS)   A special network node containing one or more MODEMs. The ACS allows users on the LAN to communicate with other LANs, BBSs, and on-line services. An ACS also allows off-site employees to dial into the LAN to upload/download files, use application programs, or read EMail.

bindery   The set of files used to store network-specific configuration information on a NetWare network. These files contain user data, security information, and other network configuration data. You cannot start the file server without this information. Corruption of any of these files can prevent the network from starting properly as well.

cache buffers   A term that refers to the smallest storage elements in a cache (an area of RAM devoted to storing commonly used pieces of information normally stored on the hard drive). Think of each buffer as a box that can store a single piece of information. The more buffers (boxes) you have, the greater the storage capacity of the cache.

CBT *See* computer-based training.

CD-ROM   Compact Disk Read-Only Memory. A device used to store up to 650 Mb of permanent data. You cannot use a CD-ROM the same as a hard or floppy disk drive because you cannot write to it. The disks look much like audio CDs but require a special drive to interface with a computer.

central configuration   The files required to tell an application, operating system, or application environment how to configure itself to interact with the user's workstation. This file might also contain user preferences like screen colors or macros. Usually these files appear on the local hard drive of each user's workstation. However, in a central configuration the files appear in one place on the file server's hard drive.

Certified NetWare Administrator (CNA)   The Certified NetWare Administrator is Novell's entry-level certification. It is for the person who needs to administer a network on a day-to-day basis. Usually these people work for one company and perform the administrator tasks in concert with their other duties. (See chapter 1 for more details.)

Certified NetWare Engineer (CNE)   The Certified NetWare Engineer is Novell's intermediate-level certification. This certification is for people who require a higher level of expertise than a system administrator. Many people who obtain the CNE certification are consultants, system integrators, or employees of companies that need a person with more skill and knowledge to help maintain the overall network. (See chapter 1 for more details.)

Certified NetWare Instructor (CNI)   The Certified NetWare Instructor is Novell's advanced-level certification. This certification is for the individual who wants to teach certified NetWare courses. These courses are taught at Novell Authorized Education Centers (NAECs) and use the Novell courseware. (See chapter 1 for more details.)

channel service unit (CSU)   A device used to terminate a dataphone digitial service (DDS) communications line. Terminating the line reduces noise and signal variances that could interfere with communications. A CSU is used for T-1 communications.

character mode interface   A menu or other application selection system that uses ASCII characters to display information. The menuing system keeps the workstation's video adapter in character mode, rather than using the display adapter's graphics mode. All line drawing characters are part of the extended ASCII character set.

CNA   *See* Certified NetWare Administrator.

CNE   *See* Certified NetWare Engineer.

CNI   *See* Certified NetWare Instructor.

common user access (CUA)   A technique for creating application menus in such a way that applications requiring similar functions use similar menus. For example, the File menu on every application will contain a Quit option. It also determines the order in which entries appear. For example, the File menu is always the first menu on the left side of the menu bar while Help is the last menu on the right side of the menu bar.

computer-based training (CBT)   An alternative means of receiving Novell training. This method uses a combination of manuals, on-screen lessons, and simulated tests to help the candidate prepare for certification exams.

CRC   *See* cyclic redundancy code.

CSU   *See* channel service unit.

CUA   *See* common user access.

cyclic redundancy code (CRC)   A technique used to ensure the reliability of information stored on hard drives, transported across network cabling, or sent from one place to another. It uses a cyclic calculation to create a numeric check number. The computer performs the same calculation when it retrieves the data and compares it to the CRC. If the two match, there is no data error. Otherwise, the sending machine must either resend the data or the receiving computer must reconstruct it.

DAT drive   Digital audiotape drive. A tape drive that uses a cassette to store data. The cassette and drive use the same technology as the audio version of the DAT drive. However, the internal circuitry of the drive formats the tape for use with a computer system. The vendor must design the interface circuitry with computer needs in mind as well. DAT allows you to store large amounts of information in a relatively small amount of space. Typical drive capacities range from 1.2 Gb to 8 Gb.

data grade line   A specially constructed telephone line that uses higher quality media and less multiplexing to reduce overall line noise and increase reliability. Data grade lines usually use fiber-optic connections to ensure a minimum of disruption from external signal sources.

data service unit (DSU)   A device, similar to a modem, that connects a PC or terminal to a dataphone digitial service (DDS) communications line. One end of the DSU connects to the terminal through a standard serial port. The other end of the DSU connects through the CSU to the four-wire DDS line. A DSU is used for T-1 communications.

DDE   *See* dynamic data exchange.

dial-in/dial-out connectivity   This is a service that allows employees to call the company network from a remote location and use the network's services. For example, if someone needed to use the company EMail system to check their incoming mail or create messages for other people in the company, they could use this service. This type of service also allows satellite offices to update or download information from the company database. The dial-out portion of the service allows people within the company to send faxes or to call on-line services using the company modem. There are a number of other uses for dial-in/dial-out connectivity.

dirty power   Electricity that contains impure elements, such as power spikes or noise. These impure elements can damage computer equipment by momentarily driving the component beyond its specified limits. Spikes usually occur as the result of motor starts and stops. Switches and other devices that change the flow of electricity can also cause spikes. Noise usually comes from electric lighting, transformers, or other devices that produce radio-frequency signals.

disk cache   A technique that increases the apparent speed of a hard disk drive by storing some of the data in RAM. There are many methods that disk cache software uses to determine which data remains in RAM. The caching technique determines how much of a speed increase you see from the disk cache.

downsizing   The process of moving applications from a large centralized mainframe/minicomputer environment to a decentralized PC LAN environment. Downsizing can involve using the mainframe/minicomputer as a database host or storage device. All user interface, security, print, and EMail functions reside on the local PC LAN. Many large businesses use downsizing as a means for reducing operating costs. A typical PC LAN requires less resources to install and maintain than a mainframe/minicomputer with similar capacity.

Drake testing center   The only company authorized by Novell to administer your certification examinations. This company specializes in providing quiet and comfortable test centers that cater to a wide range of specialties including CPAs and registered nurses. The next time you fly, you will fly with a pilot tested by a Drake testing center. (See chapter 1 for more details about the Drake testing centers.) Appendix A provides a telephone number you can use to contact the Drake testing center.

DSU   *See* data service unit.

dynamic data exchange (DDE)   The ability to cut data found in one application and paste it into another application. For example, cutting a graphic image created by a paint program and pasting it into a word processing application as part of a word processing document. Once pasted, the data does not reflect changes made to it by the originating application.

ECC *See* error checking and correcting.

ECNE *See* Enterprise Certified NetWare Engineer.

emoticon A figure created with the symbols on a keyboard. To read an emoticon, tilt your head to the left and visualize the person's expression. Use emoticons to convey the intent behind a humorous or tongue-in-cheek comment.

enhanced mode A Windows operating mode that supports the capabilities of the 80386 and higher processors. This means that Windows will use any extended memory found in the workstation by using the processor's protected mode. This mode also fully supports the virtual memory capabilities of the 80386, which means the size of the hard disk's swap file plus the amount of physical RAM determines the amount of memory available for applications. You also receive the full multitasking capabilities of the 80386 using this mode.

Enterprise Certified NetWare Engineer (ECNE) The Enterprise Certified NetWare Engineer is Novell's advanced intermediate-level certification. This certification is a continuation of the CNE program. A person who becomes an ECNE usually has some special requirements or interest in the advanced or specialized areas of networking. For example, a consultant or a network administrator might need to connect NetWare and UNIX using TCP/IP and NFS or create a wide area network using Novell's dial-in/dial-out products. (See chapter 1 for more details.)

error checking and correcting (ECC) This term originally referred to a self-diagnostic technique used to correct errors in RAM. The term now includes the same type of diagnostics provided with tape, hard disk, and floppy disk drives. In all cases the device uses some type of microcode contained in a peripheral chip to detect and correct soft errors in the data stream.

extended attribute (EA) file An OS/2 system file that stores the icon and other descriptive information about a particular data file or application. Extended attributes include long file names and the position within the workplace shell as well. Damage to the EA file usually results in a lack of descriptive information, but no loss in application functionality.

FAT *See* file allocation table disk format.

file allocation table (FAT) disk format The method of formatting a hard disk drive used by DOS and other operating systems. This technique is one of the oldest formatting methods available.

file server The centralized storage area for files and applications. Special features of the NOS enable the file server to control access to these files and applications. This allows several people to share the same file and/or application without damage to the data. A file server usually contains larger hard drives and more memory than a standard workstation. It also provides access to one or more printers. The user perceived capabilities of a file server depend on a combination of available hardware and NOS capabilities.

file statistic   Facts about one or more files on the network. These statistics can include the creation and last update dates, who created the file, who owns the file, when someone last accessed the file, who has access to it, and which user last updated it. Other statistics might include the number of file accesses, any security restrictions, or other pertinent file information.

filter condition   A Boolean (logical) statement that allows some part of the whole to pass. Think of a filter condition as you would any other filter. For example, a coffee filter allows the brewed coffee to pass, but retains the coffee grounds.

graphical user interface (GUI)   A system of icons and graphic images that replace the character mode menu system used by many machines. The GUI can ride on top of another operating system (like DOS and UNIX) or reside as part of the operating system itself (like OS/2). Advantages of a GUI are ease of use and high-resolution graphics. Disadvantages are higher workstation hardware requirements and lower performance over a similar system using a character mode interface.

graphics workstation   A PC specifically designed for graphics-oriented work. Many workstations of this type use the UNIX operating system, although they might use OS/2 or Windows as alternatives. Tektronics and many other companies make these high-performance workstations for graphic artists or draftsmen.

GUI   *See* graphical user interface.

HDLC   *See* high-level data link control.

high-level data link control (HDLC)   A standard communication line protocol developed by the International Standards Organization (ISO). The protocol defines how two devices talk to each other. Think of the protocol as a type of language used by the two devices.

high-performance file system (HPFS)   The method of formatting a hard disk drive used by OS/2. While it provides significant speed advantages over other formatting techniques, only the OS/2 operating system and applications designed to work with that operating system can access a drive formatted using this technique.

HPFS   *See* high-performance file system.

icon   A symbol used to graphically represent the purpose and/or function of an application or file. For example, text files might appear as sheets of paper with the name of the file below the icon. Applications designed for the environment or operating system usually appear with a special icon depicting the vendor's or product's logo. Icons normally appear as part of a GUI environment or operating system such as Windows or OS/2 .(See the screen shot in chapter 3 for examples of icons.)

IPX   Internet Packet Exchange. This is NetWare's peer-to-peer communication protocol. It describes a set of rules that allows two nodes to talk to each other. Think of this as the language used on the network. If everyone speaks the same language, then all the nodes can understand each other. Messages are exchanged in the form of packets on a network. Think of a packet as one sheet of a letter. There is a letterhead saying who sent the letter, an introduction saying who the letter is for, and a message that tells the receiving party what the sending party wants to say.

logic analyzer   A device that receives clock or other internal computer signals and interprets them. The resulting output is a display of the line logic. In many cases an analysis of the logic between two components will show whether the circuitry is operating correctly. A technician might also use this data to interpret the content of the information the chips transmit between themselves.

loopback plug   A device used to transfer signals from the output side of a computer port to the input side. A loopback plug allows the network administrator to test an entire serial or parallel port. Without a loopback plug, the administrator might only test the port internal circuitry. There are also loopback plugs for various NICs and other interface devices. (See chapter 11.)

memory footprint   The amount of memory used by an application once it loads and initializes itself. In some cases an application requires more memory to load than to reside in memory. TSRs usually require more memory to load than to remain in memory. This is especially true when loading a TSR into high memory.

multiprotocol router   A device used to connect two LANs together. The router moves signals from one LAN to the other. The difference between a standard router and a multiprotocol router is that the multiprotocol router can move signals between dissimilar LANS. For example, a multiprotocol router can move data between a Token Ring LAN and an ethernet LAN.

multitasking   The ability of some processor and operating environment/system combinations to perform more than one task at a time. The applications appear to run simultaneously. For example, you can download messages from an on-line service, print from a word processor, and recalculate a spreadsheet all at the same time. Each application receives a slice of time before the processor moves on to the next application. Because the time slices are fairly small, it appears to the user as if these actions are occurring simultaneously.

multithreading   This is an operating system-specific technique for breaking one or more application tasks into multiple threads of execution. Using this technique allows the operating system to devote more resources to higher priority tasks, increasing perceived system performance. The programmer must write the application to take advantage of this operating system feature when available.

NAEC   *See* Novell Authorized Test Center.

NetWare Support Encyclopedia   The NetWare Support Encyclopedia contains a complete set of Novell manuals along with articles and other information that the certified individual requires. The professional version of the product also contains a wide variety of product patches. Most of this additional material is available on the NetWire forum of CompuServe.

network administrator   The person most responsible for installing, maintaining, and upgrading the network used by a corporation. This includes managing system security and user needs as well as equipment needs.

network configuration plan   A plan that states current equipment status, network problem areas, fixes for those problems, and future upgrades. This plan can appear in either tabular or outline format and should fully answer the questions users have about network equipment status. The plan normally includes a map as well.

network file system (NFS)   A distributed file system developed by Sun Microsytems. NFS allows users of different operating systems, network architectures, protocols, or processor types to share data. More than 100 software vendors have licensed NFS from Sun Microsystems for use with their products. Novell offers NFS products to allow sharing of data from a Novell NetWare 3.x and 4.x to a UNIX host with NFS operational.

network interface card (NIC)   The device responsible for allowing a workstation to communicate with the file server and other workstations. It provides the physical means for creating the connection. The card plugs into an expansion slot in the computer. A cable that attaches to the back of the card completes the communication path.

network loadable module (NLM)   An executable file that loads on a NetWare 3.x/4.x file server. An NLM usually adds some capability that the entire network shares. Examples of NLMs include tape backup software, virus protection, UPS detection/management, and database servers. The NLM replaces the VAP provided in NetWare 2.x. Unlike a VAP, you can load and unload an NLM while the file server is active.

network operating system (NOS)   The operating system that runs on the file server or other centralized file/print sharing device. This operating system normally provides multiuser access capability and user accounting software in addition to other network-specific utilities.

NFS   *See* network file system.

NIC   *See* network interface card.

NLM   *See* network loadable module.

node   A single element in a network. In most cases the term node refers to a single workstation connected to the network. It can also refer to a bridge, router, or file server. It does not refer to cabling, passive, or active elements that do not directly interface with the network at the logical level.

NOS   *See* network operating system.

Novell Authorized Education Center (NAEC)   A training facility authorized by Novell to train CNA, CNE, ECNE, and CNI candidates in the latest network operating system technology. An NAEC always uses Certified NetWare Instructors (CNIs). It is the only place where you can receive training guaranteed to help you pass your Novell certification examinations. (See chapter 1 for more details about NAECs.)

NSE   *See* NetWare Support Encyclopedia.

object linking and embedding (OLE)   The process of packaging a file name, application name, and any required parameters into an object, then pasting this object into the file created by another application. For example, you could place a graphic object within a word processing document or spreadsheet. When you look at the object it appears as if you simply pasted the data from the originating application into the current application (similar to DDE). The data provided by the object automatically changes as you change the data in the original object. Often you can start the originating application and automatically load the required data by double-clicking on the object.

OJT   *See* on-the-job training.

OLE   *See* object linking and embedding.

on-the-job training (OJT)   A method of training where you learn by doing the tasks you want to perform. Each mistake you make and correct helps you understand another area of the job. Often this form of training is supplemented with advice from other people who know how to perform the work. This method works well for simple tasks. It does not work well for learning the principles of network operating systems. However, it is an important part of the post-training learning process.

operating system (OS)   The software that forms the computer interface between the user and the hardware. The operating system normally provides some type of command processor along with low-level functions used by applications. The user sees these low-level services as the ability to send data to the printer or receive information about a file on the hard drive. The operating system also schedules tasks, maintains the file system, and provides many vital security features.

OS   *See* operating system.

password protection   An operating system-enforced technique for restricting access to a network or data. The user must enter characters, numbers, and/or special symbols in the correct sequence before the operating system will allow access.

policies and procedures document   A set of written guidelines that the network user can refer to in case of emergency. This document also outlines the network rules and regulations. In addition, it contains the procedures for performing specific network-related tasks. (See chapter 1.)

print queue   The network version of a print spooler. It spools all print jobs for a particular printer to a network drive or the drive of a print server. Local workstation performance is not affected by a print queue. The print queue uses file or print server CPU cycles to perform its work.

print spooler   A special program that intercepts data going to the printer and places it in RAM or on disk. Once the application sending the data completes its work, the print spooler looks for clock cycles where the computer is not performing useful work. The print spooler sends some of the "spooled" data to the printer every time it sees an empty time slot. Using this technique makes it appear that the application has printed all the data when it really hasn't. The end result is that you regain control of the computer faster than if you have to wait for the printer. It also means that you use machine resources more efficiently.

printer control sequences   A set of special control character sequences that force a printer into a specific setup. For example, one set of control characters might select a special font while another set changes the print margins. The manual that comes with your printer will provide further details about what these control character sequences are and how to use them.

protocol analyzer   A device used to interpret the communication packets sent between nodes on a network. Think of the protocol analyzer as a spy reading a letter addressed to someone else before they get to see it. A protocol analyzer allows consultants and network administrators to find communication errors on the network quickly. (See chapter 12.)

RAID   Redundant array of inexpensive disks systems. A set of interconnected drives that reside outside the file server in most cases. There are several levels of RAID. Each level defines precisely how the data is placed on each of the drives. In all cases, all the drives in a group share responsibility for storing the data. They act in parallel to both read and write the data. In addition, there is a special drive in most of these systems devoted to helping the network recover when one drive fails. In most cases the user never even knows that anything has happened, the "spare drive" takes over for the failed drive without any noticeable degradation in network operation. RAID systems increase network reliability and throughput.

real mode   A Windows operating mode that supports the capabilities of the 8088/8086 processor. This essentially limits you to loading one application within the confines of conventional memory. Windows versions after 3.0 do not support this mode. You must use these versions with workstations containing an 80286 or higher processor.

router   A device used to connect two LANs together. The router moves signals from one LAN to the other.

SCSI   Small computer system interface adapter (controller). A computer interface card that allows you to connect up to seven devices to the computer system. The current SCSI standard is SCSI-2. Typical SCSI devices include tape drives, hard disk drives, and CD-ROM drives. SCSI devices typically provide high transfer rates (10 to 15 Mb/s) and access times (device-type dependent).

SDLC   *See* synchronous data link control.

shell   A command processor that allows you to directly interact with the operating system. For example, COMMAND.COM is the command processor for DOS. This also refers to menuing systems or environments that perform essentially the same task as the command processor.

sort order   A method of classifying and ordering a list of items. For example, you could place them in alphanumeric order where A would come before B and so forth.

SPX   Sequential packet exchange. This is the part of the NetWare shell that guarantees delivery of a message sent from one node to another. Think of SPX as the postal clerk that delivers a certified letter from one place to another. In network terms, each page of the letter is called a packet. SPX delivers the letter one page at a time to the intended party.

standard mode   A Windows operating mode that supports the capabilities of the 80286 processor. This means that Windows will use any extended memory found in the workstation by using the processor's protected mode. You can also load more than one application at a time (up to the limits imposed by physical RAM). This mode does not support virtual memory or page swapping. It also does not support the multitasking features of the 80386.

static interface   A menu that does not automatically change to reflect the current machine configuration or operating system environment.

synchronous data link control (SDLC)   A standard communication line protocol developed by International Business Machines (IBM). The protocol defines how two devices talk to each other. Think of the protocol as a type of language used by the two devices. This particular protocol was designed to work with Systems Network Architecture (SNA), a network architecture developed by IBM.

TCP/IP   *See* transmission control protocol/internet protocol.

terminal emulation software   A form of communications software used to connect a PC to a host. The host can take the form of a LAN, mainframe, or minicomputer. Terminal emulation software can consist of a specially designed program or a standard off-the-shelf package like Procomm Plus.

terminate and stay resident (TSR) program   An application that loads itself into memory and stays there once you execute it. The program usually returns you directly to the DOS prompt after loading. Pressing a hot-key combination activates the application, allowing you to use the application. In most cases, TSRs provide some type of utility, print spooling, or other short-term function.

transmission control protocol/internet protocol (TCP/IP)   A standard communication line protocol developed by the United States Department of Defense. The protocol defines how two devices talk to each other. Think of the protocol as a type of language used by the two devices.

troubleshooting procedures   *See* policies and procedures document.

TSR   *See* terminate and stay resident program.

upsizing   The process of linking stand-alone PCs together into a LAN. Upsizing usually results when a business grows beyond the capacity to use a "sneaker" net for exchanging files. Upsizing can require the addition of a mainframe or minicomputer for storage/data manipulation purposes when using database management applications.

user questionnaire   A set of questions designed to help the user think about their needs and express them in a way that the network administrator and corporate management can understand. (See chapter 1.)

value-added process (VAP)   An executable file that loads on a NetWare 2.x file server during file server initialization. A VAP usually adds some capability that the entire network shares. Examples of VAPs include tape backup software, virus protection, UPS detection/management, and database servers. You must load a VAP during file server startup. NetWare 2.x does not allow you to unload the VAP while the file server is active. The NLM provided with NetWare 3.x alleviates this problem.

VAP   *See* value-added process.

virtual memory   The memory provided by an 80386 or above processor. It appears as physical RAM to both the operating system and any applications running on the system, but might or might not reside within physical memory. A special part of the operating system (known as the swapping mechanism) manages the memory that appears in physical RAM and within a swap file on disk. If the processor runs out of physical memory, the swapping mechanism removes the oldest data from physical memory in segments (you can view them as memory containers), known as pages, and replaces it with blank pages from the swap file on disk. When the swap file runs out of blank pages the virtual memory area is full and you must stop any unnecessary applications. If the processor requires access to data that appears on disk, the swapping mechanism removes the oldest data from physical memory, places it in the swap file, then moves the requested data from the swap file to physical memory.

workstation   The terminal provided to the user. It provides access to application programs, hardware devices, and the network. A workstation usually resides at the user's desk, but it can appear in a centralized location as well. For example, some companies provide one or more advanced technology stations in centralized locations. These workstations serve occasional graphics or engineering needs.

WORM   Write-once, read-many drive. A device that uses CD-ROM technology coupled with a multiple power-level Laser to allow the user to write to the drive one time. Once you write to the drive, you can read the data imprinted on it multiple times. Some drives allow you to correct errors by overwriting the area of the mistake and writing the corrected data to a new area of the disk. (Of course, this assumes there is additional room on the drive for the corrected data.) The main reason to use a WORM drive is archiving of data. For example, a law office could use a WORM drive to store old cases. Like the CD-ROM drive, most WORM drives limit you to 650 Mb of data storage. Some use a proprietary encoding technique that allows you to store up to 1 Gb of data.

A

Administration
  NetWare 4.0, Advanced, 158-159
  NetWare 4.0 Administrator, 158
advertising your services, 132-134
  logo, Novell logo use, 132-134
audio- and videotapes for training, 59

B

books and printed materials for training,
    58-59
  continuing education, 124-126
brochures, logo, Novell logo use, 134-
    135
business cards, logo, Novell logo use,
    134-135

C

career-enhancement through
    certification, ix, xiii, 20-24, 91-116
  advancement within your company,
    92-94
  changing jobs/companies, 104-115
    researching potential company, 105-
    106
  competing for jobs/promotions, 24
  goal-setting and advancements, 96-97,
    97
  industry trends, 23
  interviews, emphasizing your
    qualifications, 111-112
  job seeking, 104-115
  new-position creation based on
    certification, 97-102, **99**
  organization chart for typical company,
    95
  professional recognition, 21-22
  promotions, 94-97
  resume writing, 104-115
    cover letters, 106-108, **109**
    sample resumes, **112-113**, **114-115**
    tailoring the resume to audience, 108-
    111
  skills in networking, 22-23
  support from Novell, 23-24
  title changes, 102-104
CD-ROMs from Ziff publications,
    continuing education, 121
Certified NetWare administrator (CNA),
    ix, 1, 2, 10-11

checklist for certification, 10
  paperwork log, **82**
  requirements for certification, 24-26, **25**
Certified NetWare Engineer (CNE), ix, 1,
    3-4, 11
  checklist for certification, 11, **12-14**
  continuing education requirements,
    128
  paperwork log, **82-83**
  requirements for certification, 26-28,
    27
Certified NetWare Instructor (CNI), ix, 1,
    5-10
  continuing education requirements, 129
  level categories, 6
  paperwork log, **83-84**
  paperwork, special requirements, 87-88
  Train the Trainer (TTT) classes, 7
Computer Reseller News, 124
Computer Technology Review, 124
computer-based training programs, 60
consultancy following certification, xiii,
    131-147
  advertising services, 132-134
  brochures, 134-135
  business cards, 134-135
  demonstrating certification's
    advantages, 141-142
  ID card bearing certification logo, 135-
    136
  logo, Novell logo use, 132-135
  price lists, 134-135
  pricing your services, 142-143
  professionalism in work and behavior,
    143-146, **145**
  services to offer, 136-140, **137-139**, **140**
  surveying customers, **137-139**, **140**
continuing education (*see also* training
    and education), xiii, 34, 117-129
  books and printed materials, 124-126
  CD-ROMs from Ziff publication, 121
  CNE requirements for continuing
    education, 128
  CNI requirements for continuing
    education, 129
  ECNE requirements for continuing
    education, 128-129
  electronic media, 127-128
  FaxBack on-line services, 127
  keeping your certification active,
    Novell-provided information, 120

*****Boldface** page numbers refer to art

*__Boldface__ page numbers refer to art

*Boldface page numbers refer to art

STACKER®: An Illustrated Tutorial
2nd Edition
Dan Gookin

Turn your single hard disk into two with this professional guide. Updated through Stacker 3.0, it contains information not found in the manuals. You'll use such features as Express or Custom Setup for Windows and DOS; Windows Stackometer™—a set of real-time gauges showing hard disk capacity, compression ratio, and fragmentation levels. Plus, you'll use Unstack™, a time-saving utility that decompresses files and automatically returns systems to their original state. 208 pages, 50 illustrations.

ISBN 024010-8   **$19.95 Paper**

THE HANDS-ON GUIDE TO NETWORK MANAGEMENT
John Mueller, CNE, and Robert A. Williams, CNE, CNI

Here's a toolbox of power-packed network management scripts, batch files, menus, and strategies for the optimum care and feeding of your network. Mueller and Williams, both Certified Netware Engineers, explain how to customize workstations, prepare documentation, increase efficiency, design corporate databases, assign and monitor network responsibilities, run different applications and operating systems on a network, and more. 367 pages, 135 illustrations.

ISBN 043968-0   **$26.95 Paper**
ISBN 043967-2   **$39.95 hardcover**

MS-DOS® BATCH FILE PROGRAMMING
4th Edition
Ronny Richardson

Reviewers praised Richardson's previous books:
"Exhaustive and exhilarating guide . . . Give this book an A+ for utility."
—Computer Book Review
"Now, 'The .BAT Book' will set me free!!! . . . I will recommend this one."
Computer Shopper

Find command-by-command batch file explanation tables, complete DOS command summaries, and a library of practical batch file programs included on disk in this book/disk package. Updated for DOS 6.0, this book has been extensively revised to make it even more helpful to beginning and intermediate-level DOS users. 432 pages, 59 illustrations.

ISBN 052366-5   **$32.95 Paper**
ISBN 052371-1   **$39.95 Hard**

BUILD YOUR OWN PENTIUM™ PROCESSOR PC
Aubrey Pilgrim
This addition to Windcrest's bestselling "Save a Bundle Series" makes it easy for anyone to enjoy Pentium processor speed at 386 prices.

ISBN 050164-5   **$19.95 Paper**
ISBN 050163-7   **$32.95 Hard**

LAN PERFORMANCE OPTIMIZATION
Martin A. W. Nemzow

Resolve your most stubborn network performance problems with this practical resource for LAN managers and consultants. This book-disk package will help you locate and eliminate bottlenecks in local area networks quickly. The diagnostic tools provided are equally effective with Banyan Vines, Novell Netware, UB Access One, Unix, Sun NFS, IBM LAN Server, Microsoft LAN Manager, Ethernet, Token Ring, and FDDI network operating systems. 230 pages, 90 illustrations.

ISBN 024629-7 $29.95 Paper

NETWORKING WITH LANtastic®
Michael S. Montgomery

With this instructive book you'll have an easy-to-read alternative to the program documentation—a comprehensive guide to setting up and running an efficient, high-performance LANtastic network. The author describes proven techniques for sharing files, printing, and using peripherals. Focusing on ways to configure LANtastic to meet specific needs and ensure maximum productivity, he shows you how to plan and design networks, install LANtastic software, use program functions and menus, and more. 632 pages, 199 illustrations.

ISBN 042907-3 $22.95 Paper
ISBN 042906-5 $34.95 Hard

BUILD YOUR OWN 486/486SX AND SAVE A BUNDLE
2nd Edition
Aubrey Pilgrim

This hands-on guide makes it possible for you to build your own state-of-the-art, 100% IBM-compatible PC for about one-third the retail cost or less with little more than a few parts, a screwdriver, and a pair of pliers. So don't shell out huge sums of money for a PC at your local retail outlet. This book will allow you to enjoy the speed and power of a 486—and still put food on the table. 256 pages, 58 illustrations.

ISBN 050110-6 $19.95 Paper
ISBN 050109-2 $29.95 Hard

BUILD YOUR OWN MULTIMEDIA PC
Aubrey Pilgrim

How to build a complete multimedia system—no experience required. CD-ROM, MIDI, PC sound, PCTV, voice recognition, automated speech, presentation graphics, telecommunications, and more, at the lowest possible prices. Bundled CD-ROM contains multimedia shareware.

ISBN 050113-0 $36.95 Paper

FIND IT ONLINE!
Robert I. Berkman

The consumer's guide to online computer databases and how to use them to uncover information on just about any subject. Provides practical techniques for fast, easy, inexpensive research online.

ISBN 005102-X $19.95 Paper
ISBN 005101-1 $32.95 Hard

HOME OFFICE COMPUTING HANDBOOK
Editors of Home Office Computing

Packed with creative time- and money-saving tips on how to equip a home office, keep it working smoothly, and use it to your best advantage. Featuring HOC's Four-Star picks for the best home PC hardware and software products.

ISBN 030019-4   **$19.95 Paper**

VIRTUAL REALITY: Through the new looking glass
Ken Pimentel & Keven Teixeira
Foreword by Gordon E. Moore, Chairman, Intel Corporation

Explore places that are not just uncharted, they're waiting to be created. This is the first truly accessible, easy-to-read introduction to this exciting new universe known as "cyberspace." No longer just a figment of hyperactive imaginations, the ability to experience firsthand the sights, sounds, and textures of worlds generated entirely by computer will soon be possible for almost all PC users. 335 pages, 148 illustrations.

ISBN 063409-2   **$22.95 Paper**
ISBN 063410-6   **$32.95 Hard**

EASY MULTIMEDIA: Sound and Video for the PC Crowd
Ori Gurewich/Nathan Gurewich

This book shows how to put multimedia to work in applications that feature full-motion video, sound and sound recording, colorful animation, and much more. Disk includes utilities and sample business presentations.

ISBN 025258-0   **$24.95 Paper**
ISBN 025257-2   **$34.95 Hard**

UPGRADE YOUR COMPUTER PRINTER AND SAVE A BUNDLE
Horace W. LaBadie, Jr.

Explore the affordable upgrade opportunities available for several popular printer makes and models, including Apple LaserWriters, the Hewlett-Packard Series, HP DeskJet, Canon Bubble Jets, Okidata, and others. You'll look at added font and graphics capabilities, spoolers and buffers, printer sharing and network boxes, interface converters, and caching drives, as well as software solutions such as PostScript and others. 288 pages, 245 illustrations.

ISBN 035837-0   **$19.95 Paper**
ISBN 035836-2   **$29.95 Hard**

TROUBLESHOOTING AND REPAIRING
PC DRIVES AND MEMORY SYSTEMS
Stephen J. Bigelow

Professional diagnostic techniques for IBM-compatible hard and floppy drives, tape backups, memory chips, solid-state memory cards, and optical drives (including CD-ROMs). Covers new tools, test equipment, and diagnostic software.

ISBN 005314-6   **$22.95 Paper**
ISBN 005313-8   **$39.95 Hard**

CANNED CODE FOR DOS AND WINDOWS

Steve Rimmer

  Instant solutions to the top 100 programming challenges. Packed with no-fuss code for easy data and graphics manipulation, system configuration, disk and memory management, telecommunications, printing, peripheral control, and more. Companion disk contains all the book's code—plus Graphics Workshop for Windows.

ISBN 053003-3   **$29.95 Paper**
ISBN 053002-5   **$39.95 Hard**